OPPOSING
VIEWPOINTS®
SERIES

Cybercrime

Other Books of Related Interest:

Opposing Viewpoints Series

Bioterrorism

Civil Liberties

The Music Industry

Netiquette and Online Ethics

At Issue Series

Cyberpredators

What Is the Future of the Music Industry?

What Is the Impact of Twitter?

WikiLeaks

Current Controversies Series

E-books

Espionage and Intelligence

Politics and Media

Violence in the Media

"Congress shall make
no law . . . abridging
the freedom of speech,
or of the press."

First Amendment to the US Constitution

The basic foundation of our democracy is the First Amendment guarantee of freedom of expression. The Opposing Viewpoints series is dedicated to the concept of this basic freedom and the idea that it is more important to practice it than to enshrine it.

OPPOSING
VIEWPOINTS®
SERIES

| Cybercrime

Louise I. Gerdes, Book Editor

GREENHAVEN PRESS
A part of Gale, Cengage Learning

GALE
CENGAGE Learning·

Detroit • New York • San Francisco • New Haven, Conn • Waterville, Maine • London

Elizabeth Des Chenes, *Director, Publishing Solutions*

© 2013 Greenhaven Press, a part of Gale, Cengage Learning.

Gale and Greenhaven Press are registered trademarks used herein under license.

For more information, contact:
Greenhaven Press
27500 Drake Rd.
Farmington Hills, MI 48331-3535
Or you can visit our Internet site at gale.cengage.com

For product information and technology assistance, contact us at

Gale Customer Support, 1-800-877-4253
For permission to use material from this text or product, submit all requests online at
www.cengage.com/permissions

Further permissions questions can be emailed to permissionrequest@cengage.com

Articles in Greenhaven Press anthologies are often edited for length to meet page requirements. In addition, original titles of these works are changed to clearly present the main thesis and to explicitly indicate the author's opinion. Every effort is made to ensure that Greenhaven Press accurately reflects the original intent of the authors. Every effort has been made to trace the owners of copyrighted material.

Cover Image copyright © Phecsone/Shutterstock.com.

LIBRARY OF CONGRESS CATALOGING-IN-PUBLICATION DATA

Cybercrime / Louise I. Gerdes, book editor.
    pages cm. -- (Opposing viewpoints)
    Includes bibliographical references and index.
    ISBN 978-0-7377-6312-6 (hardcover) -- ISBN 978-0-7377-6313-3 (pbk.)
    1. Computer crimes. I. Gerdes, Louise I., 1953-, editor.
    HV6773.C9123 2012
    364.16'8--dc23
                                                              2012027207

Printed in the United States of America
1 2 3 4 5 6 7 16 15 14 13 12

Contents

Chapter 3: Is Internet Activism a Cybercrime?

Chapter 4: What Laws Will Best Prevent Cybercrime?

Why Consider Opposing Viewpoints?

> *"The only way in which a human being can make some approach to knowing the whole of a subject is by hearing what can be said about it by persons of every variety of opinion and studying all modes in which it can be looked at by every character of mind. No wise man ever acquired his wisdom in any mode but this."*
>
> *John Stuart Mill*

In our media-intensive culture it is not difficult to find differing opinions. Thousands of newspapers and magazines and dozens of radio and television talk shows resound with differing points of view. The difficulty lies in deciding which opinion to agree with and which "experts" seem the most credible. The more inundated we become with differing opinions and claims, the more essential it is to hone critical reading and thinking skills to evaluate these ideas. Opposing Viewpoints books address this problem directly by presenting stimulating debates that can be used to enhance and teach these skills. The varied opinions contained in each book examine many different aspects of a single issue. While examining these conveniently edited opposing views, readers can develop critical thinking skills such as the ability to compare and contrast authors' credibility, facts, argumentation styles, use of persuasive techniques, and other stylistic tools. In short, the Opposing Viewpoints Series is an ideal way to attain the higher-level thinking and reading skills so essential in a culture of diverse and contradictory opinions.

In addition to providing a tool for critical thinking, Opposing Viewpoints books challenge readers to question their own strongly held opinions and assumptions. Most people form their opinions on the basis of upbringing, peer pressure, and personal, cultural, or professional bias. By reading carefully balanced opposing views, readers must directly confront new ideas as well as the opinions of those with whom they disagree. This is not to argue simplistically that everyone who reads opposing views will—or should—change his or her opinion. Instead, the series enhances readers' understanding of their own views by encouraging confrontation with opposing ideas. Careful examination of others' views can lead to the readers' understanding of the logical inconsistencies in their own opinions, perspective on why they hold an opinion, and the consideration of the possibility that their opinion requires further evaluation.

Evaluating Other Opinions

To ensure that this type of examination occurs, Opposing Viewpoints books present all types of opinions. Prominent spokespeople on different sides of each issue as well as well-known professionals from many disciplines challenge the reader. An additional goal of the series is to provide a forum for other, less known, or even unpopular viewpoints. The opinion of an ordinary person who has had to make the decision to cut off life support from a terminally ill relative, for example, may be just as valuable and provide just as much insight as a medical ethicist's professional opinion. The editors have two additional purposes in including these less known views. One, the editors encourage readers to respect others' opinions—even when not enhanced by professional credibility. It is only by reading or listening to and objectively evaluating others' ideas that one can determine whether they are worthy of consideration. Two, the inclusion of such viewpoints encourages the important critical thinking skill of objectively evaluating an author's credentials and bias. This evaluation will illuminate an author's reasons for taking a particular stance on an issue and will aid in readers' evaluation of the author's ideas.

It is our hope that these books will give readers a deeper understanding of the issues debated and an appreciation of the complexity of even seemingly simple issues when good and honest people disagree. This awareness is particularly important in a democratic society such as ours in which people enter into public debate to determine the common good. Those with whom one disagrees should not be regarded as enemies but rather as people whose views deserve careful examination and may shed light on one's own.

Thomas Jefferson once said that "difference of opinion leads to inquiry, and inquiry to truth." Jefferson, a broadly educated man, argued that "if a nation expects to be ignorant and free . . . it expects what never was and never will be." As individuals and as a nation, it is imperative that we consider the opinions of others and examine them with skill and discernment. The Opposing Viewpoints series is intended to help readers achieve this goal.

David L. Bender and Bruno Leone,
Founders

Introduction

> "Both hero and antihero, the hacker is both cause and remedy of social crises."
>
> —Douglas Thomas,
> professor of cultural studies
> of technology and author of
> Hacker Culture

While people may generally agree how to define a crime, they often disagree on who is a criminal. In the eyes of some, criminal intent is an important consideration. The fictional Robin Hood, who robbed from the rich and gave to the poor, was an enemy of the state but a hero among the people. Those imprisoned for treasonous political beliefs may be criminals in the eyes of their governments but heroes to the people whose causes they support. Some legal philosophers argue that criminals who break the law for gain or personal gratification hope to hide their acts, while political criminals thrive on publicity to generate sympathy and legitimacy. This latter view, the idea that common criminals, unlike political activists, want anonymity, would make criminals of all computer hackers whether they hacked for profit or not. Hacking—the use of advanced knowledge of computer systems to surreptitiously enter the computers or networks of others without permission—is by its very nature an anonymous activity.

Many in the information technology and security community, however, believe that anonymous hacking for good is not, and should not be, criminal. In fact, at the annual DEF CON computer hackers' convention in 2011, the social networking company Facebook offered attendees a minimum of $500 to hack into its website and expose its security flaws. Agents of cyber-defense units of federal agencies, including the Federal Bureau of Investigation (FBI) and the Pentagon, also attend the convention, not with the goal of arresting hackers—although there have been arrests and legal actions against hackers at DEF CON in the past—but to learn how hackers might expose security flaws in critical American infrastructure and defense systems. Jeff Moss, DEF CON's founder, characterizes Facebook's bounty program and the sale of hacking discoveries to vulnerable businesses as a vulnerability economy, in which security-flaw discoveries become a product and hackers become producers. Thus, while hacking poses a threat for some, for those seeking to close security vulnerabilities, hacking is beneficial. Indeed, distinguishing the good hackers from the bad is a matter of perspective, which in turn complicates the development of effective cybersecurity policies and practices. These contradictions are reflective of many cybercrime debates.

The first hackers, who appeared as early as the 1960s, were students, mainly from schools such as the Massachusetts Institute of Technology. They hacked computer networks for fun, not for profit. At the time, computers were viewed as complex tools understood only by computer experts. The word "hacker" was synonymous with computer nerd. The efforts of these early hackers led to more efficient programs, and many hackers went on to be successful technology entrepreneurs. In fact, one of these early hackers was Stephen Gary Wozniak, Apple Computer's cofounder. Many of these early hackers believed that software and hardware programming code should be free and widely distributed so that it could be improved on by those who use it. Technology writer Steven Levy, in his book *Hackers: Heroes of the Computer Revolution*, identifies this as the hacker ethic. The hacker ethic also opposes corporate or government control over technology. Indeed, over the years, the tension between these early hackers and corporate and government interests grew.

Not all analysts in computer technology's early years believed in the hacker ethic or that hacking without a malicious motive was benign. Some, particularly companies and government agencies that wanted their computers to be secure, viewed hackers not as computer nerds but as potential threats. Thus, in 1984 Congress passed the Counterfeit Access Device and Computer Fraud and Abuse Act. However, some law enforcement analysts argued the law lacked teeth and reflected a lack of understanding about the true nature of computer technology. Loopholes in the 1984 legislation prohibited prosecution of those who simply used a computer without authorized access, even if the hacker had viewed unauthorized data. Moreover, the law required proof that access was unauthorized, which prevented the prosecution of employees, even if their use was malicious. In fact, in the two years following the act's passage, the law led to only one indictment.

Congress amended the act in 1996 to allow prosecution for the unauthorized viewing of data, even if the hacker had no motive to gain financially from the hack. Indeed, although he claims that he never intended to profit from his acts, hacker Kevin Mitnick served five years in prison for his 1999 conviction for computer fraud. His arrest and conviction remain controversial. Mitnick maintains that many claimed commercial losses were invented by embarrassed businesses, and some claim that he was demonized by members of the press, who made false claims that he hacked into NORAD, the radar system designed to warn of a nuclear missile strike. Nevertheless, Mitnick remains in the eyes of many the quintessential computer criminal, and his actions brought public attention to the risks of networked computers. The public image of the benign, nerdy hacker began to shift.

By the late 1990s, the role of the computer had changed from its early use as a research tool. Computers were by that time running vast financial, infrastructure, and governance systems. The number of personal computers in homes had also grown significantly as had access to the Internet. According to professor and *Hacker Culture* author Douglas Thomas, "Kids got computers under the Christmas tree that they couldn't open up." Thus, unlike the early hackers, they could not tinker with the computers themselves. "So," Thomas claims, "instead of exploring computers, they started exploring network connections." University of Dayton law professor Susan W. Brenner agrees that the change in computer hacking is "not a sign that American adolescents are more unprincipled than they used to be," but evidence of the computer's changing role. When hackers in the late 1980s through the 1990s began to access government and corporate networks, the government response was strong, and the image of the good-guy hacker began to fade for many. People wanted their identities, their money, and their privacy protected. However, for those who saw computers as a tool of government oppression, the hacker remained a hero. Indeed, Hollywood continued to frame the hacker as a Robin Hood–like hero in movies such as *The Matrix*. Thus, in the new millennium, the use of computers became more widespread and the technology more complex. The way people viewed hacking, in turn, often led to conflicting attitudes.

In response to fears of increased government and corporate control, software developers, some of whom were once hackers, began to organize to protect hacker civil liberties. The Electronic Frontier Foundation (EFF), for example, provides legal representation and lobbies for user rights. In July 2005, it defended Mike Lynn, one of the new breed of hackers who call themselves security researchers. These hackers formed, or were employed by, cybersecurity companies whose objective is to identify security flaws in computer network systems. Cisco Systems, a large technology firm, claimed that Lynn had violated the company's copyrights by agreeing to speak at a Black Hat technical security conference about security flaws that he had found in routers manufactured by Cisco. Although Cisco discovered and fixed the flaw in April 2005, it did not inform its users of the problem's severity. Cisco obtained a court order to prevent Lynn from speaking about the flaw at the convention. Lynn agreed, but when he began his talk on another topic, the audience began to boo him, so he proceeded to deliver the original presentation. Despite EFF efforts, the case was settled with a permanent injunction, and Lynn was never to discuss his discovery.

The line between good-guy and bad-guy hackers became further blurred in 2011 when hacking became a form of protest called hacktivism. Groups such as Anonymous and Lulz Security, or LulzSec, masterminded hacking protests against government and corporate websites whose policies they opposed. In the eyes of some hacking-culture analysts, hacktivism is not really good-guy hacking in the purest sense, as hacktivist protests are not designed to innovate or improve technology—part of the original hacker ethic. Nevertheless, hacktivists do not profit, and they participate voluntarily. Thus, hacktivism creates a new hacker gray area. Although profit is not a hacktivist's goal, some attacks have been controversial. In August 2011, San Francisco Bay Area Rapid Transit (BART) officials blocked underground cell phone service to prevent protesters from using social networking to organize a demonstration over the fatal shooting of a forty-five-year-old man by police. Some criticized BART's decision, questioning whether the move violated free speech. Anonymous responded by posting the names, phone numbers, and street and e-mail addresses of BART website subscribers. The hacktivist organization confirmed its responsibility in an online post: "We are Anonymous, we are your citizens, we are the people, we do not tolerate oppression from any government agency." Although no financial information was revealed, some argued that the attack exposed the private information of innocent individuals. Indeed, victim Laura Eichman asserts, "I think what they (the hackers) did was illegal and wrong. I work in

IT [information technology] myself, and I think that this was not ethical hacking. I think this was completely unjustified."

While the criminality of the good-guy hacker and hacktivist remains subject to debate, most agree that cybercrime is a serious problem that should be addressed. Nevertheless, some question the impact and constitutionality of recommended policies. Indeed, many cybercrime debates center on how to create policies that balance the needs of victims with the need for innovation and the protection of personal rights and liberties, including those of hackers. How to balance these needs remains hotly contested as the viewpoints in the following chapters reveal. The authors of the viewpoints in *Opposing Viewpoints: Cybercrime* explore these and other issues concerning the nature and scope of Internet crime and the laws designed to address it in chapters including Is Cybercrime a Serious Problem?, How Do Cybercriminals Use Online Media to Commit Crimes?, Is Internet Activism a Cybercrime?, and What Laws Will Best Prevent Cybercrime? Whether the hacker is a cybercriminal or a cyber hero, some believe the debate is less about the hacker and more about how society feels about technology that it uses freely but knows little about. *Hacker Culture*'s Thomas concludes, "The discourse surrounding hacking reveals little about hackers themselves; instead, it tells us a great deal about social attitudes toward technology."

CHAPTER 1

Is Cybercrime
a Serious Problem?

Chapter Preface

The United States is one of the most wired nations in the world. In fact, each year more Americans become dependent on the Internet; accompanying this growing dependence is a growth in cybercrime. "As the number of people with access to the Internet increases every year, multijurisdictional and multinational cyber[crime] cases continue to grow at an exponential rate," maintains Michael P. Merritt, assistant director of the US Secret Service's Office of Investigations. To combat computer crime, as early as 1984 Congress passed the Counterfeit Access Device and Computer Fraud and Abuse Act. In the years since, as the acts of cybercriminals grow more sophisticated, government and law enforcement struggle to keep up. While these agencies claim they are doing their best with the resources provided, other analysts argue that these efforts are inadequate and that law enforcement is losing the war on cybercrime.

Some cybersecurity experts and law enforcement officials agree that the fight against cybercrime is a daunting challenge. According to David DeWalt, president and chief executive officer of the Internet security software company McAfee, "While a lot has been done to combat cybercrime over the past decade, criminals still have the upper hand." In fact, law enforcement officials disclosed that in January 2010, hackers in Europe and China gained access to the computers of more than 2,400 companies and government agencies in 196 countries, stealing financial information, intellectual property, and trade secrets. In March 2009, Eugene Spafford, executive director of Purdue University's Center for Education and Research in Information Assurance and Security, testified before Congress that the nation has for years been persistently under attack. "Criminals and agents of foreign powers have been probing our computing systems, defrauding our citizens, stealing cutting-edge research and design materials, corrupting critical systems and snooping on government information," Spafford reveals. Few policy makers, however, have heeded these warnings, in Spafford's view. He concedes that part of the problem is that no one wants to spend the money. "There is an unwillingness to match the problem with resources," he reasons.

Those fighting cybercrime claim that this lack of resources makes it difficult to combat increasingly complex cybercrimes. "As we have seen these types of criminal cases growing in size and scope, the expertise, training, personnel, and resources needed to investigate and prosecute these cases continue to increase," Merritt argues. Indeed, the cost of fighting financial fraud on the Internet, for example, takes much longer and requires greater resources than fighting traditional fraud cases. According to Merritt, a traditional fraud case takes six months to a year to investigate and prosecute, while Internet fraud can take three to four years, thus requiring more resources. Even more daunting is the fact that some cybercrime gangs are large and well structured and have thus far escaped prosecution. According to cybersecurity columnist Roger A. Grimes, these cybercrime syndicates "have corporate headquarters that would fit the model of the Fortune 1000. They have extensive payrolls, pay millions in taxes and enjoy business growth that would be the envy of Wall Street. Yet we haven't prosecuted a single person from any of these big online cybercrime syndicates."

Whether Congress will develop the political will to devote resources to fight cybercrime depends on whether lawmakers believe the problem is serious enough to warrant these resources, a view that remains hotly contested. The authors in the following chapter explore whether cybercrime is a serious problem.

> *"Identity theft occurs to about 11 million Americans per year, resulting in some $54 billion in losses."*

Identity Theft Is a Serious Problem

Sid Kirchheimer

Identity theft is a growing problem that affects as many as eleven million Americans each year, claims Sid Kirchheimer in the following viewpoint. Many losses result from lost or stolen credit cards, while still others are the result of stolen personal information obtained by cybercriminals who hack corporate computers, he maintains. Some of the most costly losses occur when cybercriminals steal personal information to pay for surgery or medical treatments, Kirchheimer asserts. More frightening, he contends, are cases in which criminals use stolen identities to commit crimes for which the unknowing victims are charged. Kirchheimer, who writes on consumer issues for the AARP Bulletin, is the author of Scam-Proof Your Life.

As you read, consider the following questions:

1. According to Kirchheimer, how do criminals use Facebook to defraud a victim's friends?

Sid Kirchheimer, "They Stole My Name!," *Saturday Evening Post*, January/February 2011, vol. 283, no. 1, pp. 32–35. Copyright © 2011 by the Saturday Evening Post. All rights reserved. Reproduced by permission.

2. What does the author claim are the biggest causes of identity theft?

3. In the author's opinion, how many Americans admit to falling for check-forwarding schemes?

Teresa Bidwell lost her house to an identity thief. Her signature was forged on a property transfer form—available for about $10 at most office supply stores—and filed at City Hall to "prove" that her Philadelphia rental property was sold for $5,000 cash, a fraction of its value. Bidwell learned about the theft when contractors she hired to prepare the house for a new tenant arrived and discovered that another crew, hired by the new "owner," had already gutted it. "When I went to City Hall, there were maybe 20 people in the deed recorder's office, using its computers to research property records," she says. "I told the clerk, 'I'm here because my house was stolen,' and those computer users scattered like cockroaches. It took more than one year, $16,000, and a lot of hassles to get back my house."

Easy Access to Personal Information

Bryan Rutberg's identity was stolen on Facebook. Shortly after joining, his page was hacked, and a bogus message was posted stating that he had been robbed while traveling overseas and needed money to return home. He tried in vain to remove the phony plea for help, but the scammer had changed his password and "defriended" his wife, so he couldn't even view his own page. Concerned friends offered assistance, but he was unable to warn them.

Before he could regain access to his account, his identity thief used information gleaned from Rutberg's page to "prove" he was the "stranded" West Coast business executive—convincing one friend to wire $1,200. "If you're looking to impersonate someone, Facebook is a good place to start," Rutberg says. "My page had the names and photographs of my wife, kids, parents, friends, where I went to high school and college—all kinds of personal information."

Unfortunately, even after death, identity theft can occur. When Johnnie Salter died at 72, he owned two credit cards. But two weeks following his death, applications were made for 21 credit cards—and a loan taken for a new car—in his name. His identity thief scoured obituaries in local newspapers for names, dates of birth, and addresses of "victims," then bought their Social Security numbers on Web sites—routinely used by police, debt collectors, and others for "legit" purposes and unfortunately, also by scammers—to get new credit under their identities and mailed to a vacant home.

"It's bad enough to steal someone's identity and ruin their credit," notes Salter's sister, Billie Crane. "To do it to a dead man and to his family so shortly after his death is just terrible."

A Growing Trend

Identity theft occurs to about 11 million Americans per year, resulting in some $54 billion in losses, according to a February 2010 study by Javelin Strategy & Research, which conducts financial services research.

The biggest causes: bad luck or bad blood. More than one in three cases results from a lost or stolen wallet, checkbook, or credit card. In roughly 10 percent of cases, the thief is a friend, relative, coworker, or acquaintance of the victim.

But there are also corporate security breaches, in which customer files with personal information are hacked by cyber-criminals. There are mail-stealing crooks who cruise neighborhoods, pilfering incoming credit card applications, tax forms, letters from insurers, and outgoing bills with checks; corrupt store clerks who copy customers' credit card numbers for personal shopping sprees; Web sites and e-mails that unleash computer viruses that steal online files and passwords; scammers purporting to be legitimate businessmen and government officials who telephone and write with any number of stories to solicit personal information; even "moles" hired by organized scam rings to work undercover in banks, doctors' offices, and businesses—earning commissions by collecting your vital data.

The reports are alarming. However, by shining a light on the diabolically creative criminal mind, you can better understand how vulnerable you are to identity theft and what you can do to help prevent the crime from happening to you.

The per-victim loss is $4,841 for financial identity theft, such as a stolen or new credit card in the victim's name, and nearly $20,160 in fast-growing cases of medical identity theft, in which thieves impersonate someone else at a hospital or doctor's office, using stolen health insurance account numbers or personal information—such as a person's Social Security card—to get health care coverage for surgery or other treatments. Banks and credit issuers typically eat the majority of those per-account losses—if not all—but victims average about 21 hours and hundreds if not thousands of dollars out of pocket to clear their name.

A Frightening Twist

Depending on how the identity was pilfered, the victim could face another problem: being targeted as the thief himself.

That's what happened to Earl Walls, a 69-year-old retired factory supervisor in Huntington, West Virginia. When he answered an advertisement for a work-at-home job, allegedly sent by a well-known British artist named Jack Russell, who was operating a gallery, he thought he could earn easy money processing payments from customers of the artist.

The task seemed simple enough. Walls would receive checks at home, deposit them in his bank account, then send a Western Union wire transfer overseas—earning a 10 percent commission of the forwarded amount.

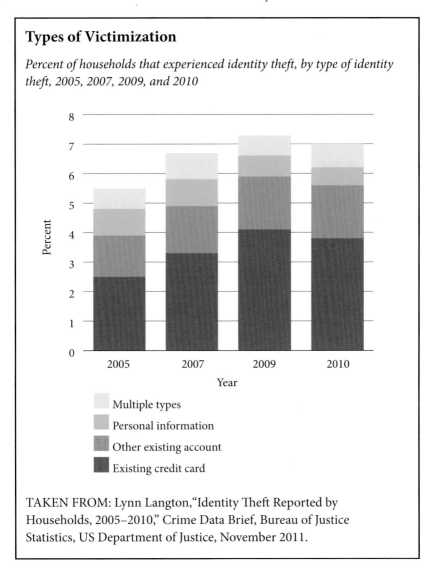

Types of Victimization

Percent of households that experienced identity theft, by type of identity theft, 2005, 2007, 2009, and 2010

Legend:
- Multiple types
- Personal information
- Other existing account
- Existing credit card

TAKEN FROM: Lynn Langton, "Identity Theft Reported by Households, 2005–2010," Crime Data Brief, Bureau of Justice Statistics, US Department of Justice, November 2011.

After providing his bank account information for direct-deposit commission payments, he received the first batch of customer checks—six traveler's checks, each for $500—and made the deposit and transfer. Eleven days later, he received another eight checks. But when he entered his bank to deposit them, he was arrested and charged with check fraud and counterfeiting.

Walls was duped in a check-forwarding scheme, a common hoax in which you receive a fake but authentic-looking check in the mail, with instructions to deposit it in your bank account and quickly forward all or a portion elsewhere, usually overseas via a wire transfer. Nearly 1.5 million Americans admit to falling for these ruses, a fraction of the likely number of victims. Often, they are "winners" of a sweepstakes or lottery who receive a "partial payment" check, and are then told to forward an amount to cover taxes or insurance before claiming their remaining windfall. However, like Walls, they face one small problem: Victims in such scams face possible arrest.

Unless it's a clear or suspected fake, the U.S. Expedited Funds Availability Act adopted in 1987 requires that deposited checks less than $5,000 be "made available" in the depositor's account within one to five days, depending on the type of check. But "made available" doesn't mean the check has cleared, no matter what the teller says or your bank account indicates. It can take a bank up to two weeks to actually collect the funds from the check issuer, until then, the bank essentially "fronts" the deposited amount, expecting that it's legitimate.

When the check proves bogus and the bank doesn't collect, you're liable for money drawn from that deposit—and possible charges.

For Earl Walls, that was $3,000—the amount wired from the first batch of deposited checks. At the bank that day, "the teller asked no questions, only had me sign each check and gave me cash," he says. "I was told everything was fine, so I went to Western Union to wire the money."

The Talk of the Town

When he entered his bank with the second batch, a manager recognized him and called police. "Earl was handcuffed in the bank lobby, in front of everybody," says family friend Felicia

Adams. After his arrest was reported in the local newspaper and his mug shot shown on TV, "he became the talk of the town . . . and not in the way you want in Smalltown, USA. He was treated like some kind of criminal mastermind." Before that, Walls "had never had so much as a traffic ticket."

Set to stand trial and facing up to 16 years in prison, charges against Walls were dropped after a reporter tracked down the "artist" who e-mailed Walls offering the phony job. In reality, he was part of a Nigerian scam ring simultaneously recruiting victims into various check-forwarding ploys under several pseudonyms, including the identity of the legitimate well-known artist. Outside the jurisdiction of U.S. law enforcement, the real criminal was never apprehended.

The stress of his scheduled trial caused Walls to be hospitalized twice with chest pains. For two months, his bank account was frozen, so the scammer couldn't do more damage to Walls' identity. But the move also blocked Walls' access to his only source of income, his direct-deposit Social Security check, forcing him to borrow money to pay his bills.

"I still break out in a cold sweat every time I see a FedEx truck on my street," he says, recalling how the phony checks were delivered. "I never knew I was doing anything wrong, but people still treat me like I'm a criminal. I was at my aunt's house recently and a neighbor asked, 'Aren't you that guy I saw on TV for being arrested?' You could tell what he thought by the way he was looking at me, like I was guilty. It's really embarrassing being taken like I was."

"In 2008, [only] 23% of identity theft victims reported suffering a personal out-of-pocket loss (direct loss, indirect loss, or both) of at least $1."

The Impact of Identity Theft for Most Victims Is Minimal

Lynn Langton and Michael Planty

In the following viewpoint, Lynn Langton and Michael Planty maintain that while identify theft is indeed a problem, most victims suffer minor losses. In fact, they assert, less than a quarter of identity theft victims suffered any out-of-pocket financial loss and, of these, over one-third lost less than $100. Moreover, Langton and Planty claim, nearly half spent one day or less resolving the problem. Based on the results of a 2008 survey, only 20 percent of identity theft victims found the experience severely distressing. Langton and Planty are statisticians for the US Department of Justice's Bureau of Justice Statistics.

As you read, consider the following questions:

1. What was the most prevalent type of identity theft in 2008, according to Langton and Planty?

Lynn Langton and Michael Planty, "Victims of Identity Theft, 2008," National Crime Victimization Survey Supplement, Bureau of Justice Statistics, Special Report, US Department of Justice, December 2010. pp. 1–5, 8.

2. According to the 4.5 million victims who knew how their identifying information had been obtained, under what circumstances did the greatest percentage believe their identity was stolen, in the authors' view?

3. In the authors' opinion, what percentage of identity theft victims reported that the identity theft caused significant problems with their job or schoolwork?

Approximately 11.7 million persons, representing 5% of all persons age 16 or older in the United States, were victims of one or more types of identity theft within a 2-year period. The most common type of identity theft, experienced by 6.2 million people during the 2-year reporting period, was the unauthorized use of an existing credit card account.

This report is based on data from the 2008 Identity Theft Supplement (ITS) to the National Crime Victimization Survey (NCVS). From January to June of 2008, the NCVS-ITS collected data from persons who had experienced one or more attempted or successful incidents of identity theft during the 2 years preceding their interviews.

In the NCVS-ITS and this report, identity theft victims include persons who experienced one or more of the following incidents:

- Unauthorized use or attempted use of an existing account, such as a credit/debit card, checking, savings, telephone, online, or insurance account.

- Unauthorized use or attempted use of personal information to open a new account, such as a credit/debit card, telephone, checking, savings, loan, or mortgage account.

- Misuse of personal information for a fraudulent purpose, such as getting medical care, a job, or government benefits; renting an apartment or house; or providing false information to law enforcement when charged with a crime or traffic violation.

This report focuses on the overall number, percentage, and demographic characteristics of victims who reported at least one type of identity theft during a 2-year period ending in 2008. It details the victims' direct and indirect financial losses; the time spent resolving problems related to the identity theft; the percentage of victims who reported the theft to credit card companies, credit bureaus, and law enforcement agencies; and the level of distress felt by identity theft victims. . . .

The Prevalence and Type of Identity Theft

In the NCVS-ITS, the unauthorized misuse or attempted misuse of an existing account was the most prevalent type of identity theft, experienced by 10.1 million persons age 16 or older (4% of all persons) over the 2-year period. The majority of victims experienced the fraudulent use of their existing credit cards (6.2 million victims or 3% of all persons) or bank accounts (4.4 million victims or 2% of all persons). Another 811,900 victims (0.3% of all persons) experienced other types of existing account theft, such as the misuse or attempted misuse of an existing telephone, online, or insurance account.

An estimated 1.7 million victims (0.7% of all persons) reported the fraudulent misuse of their information to open a new account, such as a credit card or telephone account. Another 618,900 victims (0.3% of all persons) reported the misuse of their personal information to commit other crimes, such as fraudulently obtaining medical care or government benefits or providing false information to law enforcement during a crime or traffic stop.

Many victims experienced multiple types of identity theft. About 16% of all victims (1.8 million victims) experienced multiple types of identity theft during the 2-year period. For the majority of victims of multiple types of identity theft (65%), the thefts involved unauthorized use of a combination of existing accounts, such as credit card, checking, savings, telephone, or online accounts. . . .

Victim Demographics

A similar percentage of men and women (5%) experienced identity theft during the 2-year period. The percentages of victims, when categorized by type of theft (e.g., unauthorized use of existing account information, misuse of information to open a new account, misuse of personal information for other fraudulent purposes), did not vary by gender. A greater percentage of persons ages 16 to 24 (6%) were victims of at least one type of identity theft than persons age 65 or older (4%). A greater percentage of persons living in households with an income of $75,000 or more experienced at least one type of identity theft than persons living in households with lower incomes.

Differences were observed among demographic groups in the percentage of respondents who experienced the unauthorized use of an existing account, such as a credit card or bank account. A greater percentage of persons living in households with an income of $75,000 or more (5%) experienced fraud involving an existing account than persons living in households with an income below $75,000. A greater percentage of whites (4%) than blacks (2%) experienced theft of an existing account in the 2-year period. Differences across income and race categories may be related to the prevalence and use of credit cards and bank accounts.

Recognizing Identity Theft

In 2008, 11.7 million persons had experienced one type or one incident of identity theft during the prior 2 years. Of these victims, about 40% had some idea as to how the identity theft occurred. A greater percentage of victims who experienced multiple types of identity theft in a single incident (50%) knew how the theft had occurred, compared to victims of all other types.

Of the 4.5 million victims who knew how their identifying information had been obtained, nearly 30% believed their identity was stolen during a purchase or other transaction. Another 20% believed the information was lost or stolen from a wallet or checkbook, followed by 14% who thought the information was stolen from personnel or other files at an office. Eight percent thought family or friends stole their information. However, among identity theft victims who had their personal information used for fraudulent purposes and knew how their information was obtained, about 4 in 10 (39%) thought that family or friends were responsible.

The Financial Impact

The economic impact of identity theft can be broken down into direct and indirect financial loss. Direct financial loss refers to the monetary amount the offender obtained from misusing the victim's account or personal information, including the estimated value of goods, services, or cash obtained. Indirect loss includes any other costs accrued because of the identity theft, such as legal fees, bounced checks, and other miscellaneous expenses (postage, phone calls, or notary fees).

In 2008, 62% of identity theft victims reported a direct or indirect financial loss associated with the theft during the prior 2 years. Victims of identity theft reported a cumulative financial loss of nearly $17.3 billion during the 2-year period. Across all types of identity theft, victims suffering a financial loss of at least $1 lost an average of $2,400, with a median loss of $430.

The percentage of victims who suffered any financial loss varied by the type of identity theft. Approximately 61% of victims of credit card fraud, 70% of victims of bank card fraud, 48% of new account fraud, and 24% of personal information fraud experienced a financial loss during the previous 2 years. Of those victims who experienced multiple types of

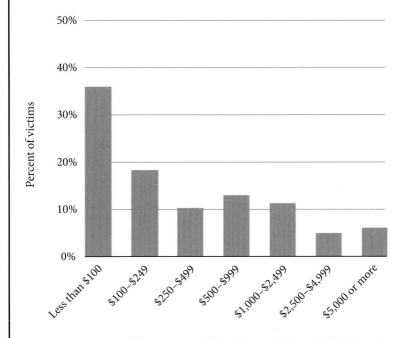

Losses from Identity Theft Are Generally Small

Total out-of-pocket loss for identity theft victims who experienced a direct or indirect financial loss from identity theft during a 2-year period, 2008

Note: Financial loss is computed from the 23% of identity theft victims who experienced a personal loss of at least $1.

TAKEN FROM: Lynn Langton and Michael Planty, "Victims of Identity Theft, 2008," National Crime Victimization Survey Supplement, Bureau of Justice Statistics, Special Report, US Department of Justice, December 2010.

identity theft, about 70% reported a financial loss. Victims of new account fraud incurred an average financial loss of $7,250, with a median loss of $802.

In some instances, a company, such as a credit card or insurance company, may reimburse some or all of the financial loss, reducing or eliminating out-of-pocket losses. In 2008,

23% of identity theft victims reported suffering a personal out-of-pocket loss (direct loss, indirect loss, or both) of at least $1. Among the victims who experienced some out-of-pocket financial loss as a result of the theft, 36% lost less than $100, and 22% lost $1,000 or more.

Direct financial loss. In 2008, about 59% of the 11.7 million victims of identity theft reported direct financial losses during the previous 2 years totaling $16.6 billion. The percentage of victims who suffered a direct financial loss varied by the type of identity theft. Approximately 59% of credit card fraud victims, 68% of bank card fraud victims, 42% of new account fraud victims, and 18% of personal information fraud victims experienced a direct financial loss during the previous 2 years. Of those victims who experienced multiple types of identity theft, about 69% reported a direct financial loss.

Of the victims who reported a direct financial loss, victims of new account fraud incurred an average direct financial loss of $8,110, with a median loss of $1,000. Victims who experienced the misuse of their personal information reported an average direct loss of $2,829 and a median direct loss of $2,500. Victims of credit card fraud (9%) had an average direct loss of $1,105 (median direct loss $400). Victims who experienced multiple types of fraud reported an average direct loss of $4,680, with a median direct loss of $600.

Approximately 16% of all victims reported direct out-of-pocket personal losses, which totaled $4.1 billion over the 2-year period. The 16% of victims who suffered a direct personal loss of at least $1 lost an average of $2,228, with a median loss of $300. A greater percentage of victims of multiple types of identity theft (26%) and victims of bank account theft (25%) experienced personal direct losses, compared with victims of credit card fraud (9%), new account fraud (5%), and the misuse of personal information (10%).

Indirect losses. In addition to any direct financial loss, approximately 11% of all identity theft victims reported indirect losses which totaled $1.04 billion over the 2-year period. The 11% of victims who suffered an indirect loss of at least $1 reported an average indirect loss of $788, with a median of $50, from dealing with the identity theft over the 2 years. With the exception of victims of fraud involving an existing account other than a credit card or bank account, victims of each type of identity theft who reported an indirect financial loss had a median indirect loss of $100 or less. Victims who experienced the fraudulent misuse of their personal information reported the largest average indirect loss of $3,955, with a $100 median loss.

At the time of the interview, 42% of victims who experienced identity theft within the prior 2 years reported spending a day or less to resolve financial or credit problems associated with the theft. For each type of identity theft, the greatest percentage of victims resolved the problem in a day or less. About 20% of reporting victims spent more than a month from the discovery of the theft trying to clear up the problems. . . .

Victim Distress

Victims who experienced a direct financial loss were asked how the identity theft affected their lives. Approximately 3% of these victims reported that the identity theft caused significant problems with their job or schoolwork, or trouble with a supervisor, coworkers, or peers. Additionally, about 6% of victims attributed significant problems with family members or friends to the identity theft victimization, including getting into more arguments or fights, not feeling that they could trust family or friends as much, or not feeling as close to family or friends as before the theft.

Victims were also asked to rate how distressing the identity theft was for them. About 11% did not find the theft distressing at all, 34% found it mildly distressing, 33% found it moderately distressing, and 20% found it severely distressing.

The impact of identity theft on the victim's work, school, and family relationships, as well as the level of distress, varied by the type of identity theft. A greater percentage of victims who experienced personal information fraud reported a direct negative impact on work or school (11%) and family relationships (13%), compared with victims who experienced the unauthorized use of a credit card (2% or less). Additionally, 30% of victims of personal information fraud reported the incident as severely distressing, compared with 11% of victims of credit card fraud.

Victims who spent more time resolving financial and credit problems resulting from the identity theft were more likely to experience severe distress than victims who cleared up the problems more quickly. Among victims who spent more than 6 months resolving problems resulting from the theft, over 40% felt the identity theft was severely distressing; less than 15% of victims who spent a day or less resolving problems found the incident severely distressing.

"While cyber defenders must confront the full range of security vulnerabilities, the cyberterrorists need to succeed in finding and exploiting only a single vulnerability to accomplish their mission."

Cyberterrorism Poses a Serious Threat to National Security

John R. Rossi

Unlike online pranksters, thieves and bullies, cyberterrorists attack computers for ideological reasons, claims John R. Rossi in the following viewpoint. Devastating attacks on Estonia's digital infrastructure demonstrate that cyberterrorism is a very real problem, he reasons. Of particular concern in the United States are those systems connected to America's critical infrastructures, Rossi asserts. Unfortunately, he maintains, many of these systems use well-known operating systems and lack tight security. Rossi warns that while those defending these networks must monitor many vulnerabilities, the cyberterrorists need only find one to cause destruction. Rossi, an information systems security expert, teaches at National Defense University and has worked on systems security with many federal agencies.

As you read, consider the following questions:

1. What examples of at-risk computer-controlled industrial controls systems does Rossi provide?

2. According to the author, what is the good news about what can be done to combat terrorism?

3. In the author's view, how does the passion of terrorists and security professionals differ?

One of the key challenges of understanding 'cyberterrorism' is defining exactly what the term means. The term has been used in the past to refer to known terrorists or terrorist organisations using the Internet to communicate.

Currently, the term cyberterrorism more often refers to the act of attempting to damage or exploit cyber networks and their connected computers or the act of attempting to use cyber networks (especially the Internet) to wreak havoc and destruction on other targets, which they access through cyber networks. Even the individual terms 'cyber' and 'terrorist' are inconsistently interpreted.

What the Experts Say

Andrew M. Colarik of the USA and Lech J. Janczewski of New Zealand state that, "In the context of information security, terrorists may come in many forms such as politically motivated, anti-government, anti–world trade, and pro–environmental extremists".

They further state, "Cyberterrorism means premeditated, politically motivated attacks by subnational groups or clandestine agents, or individuals against information and computer systems, computer programmes, and data that result in violence against noncombatant targets".

This interpretation of cyberterrorism creates a distinction between a cyberterrorist and a malicious hacker, prankster, identity thief, cyberbully, or corporate spy based on the political motivation of the attacker. It also differs from hacking, cracking, phishing, spamming, and other forms of computer-related abuse, though cyberterrorists may use these tactics to accomplish their politically motivated goals.

Dr. Dorothy Denning, professor in the Department of Defense Analysis at the Naval Postgraduate School, states that cyberterrorism "refers to the convergence of terrorism and cyberspace. It is generally understood to mean unlawful attacks and threats of attacks against computers, networks, and the information stored therein when done to intimidate or coerce a government or its people in furtherance of political and social objectives".

According to Dr. Irving Lachow, PhD, professor of systems management at the US National Defense University in Washington, D.C., "While there is clear evidence that terrorists have used the Internet to gather intelligence and coordinate efforts to launch physical attacks against various infrastructure targets, there has not been a single documented incidence of cyberterrorism against the US government."

It should also be noted that there is another school of thought that says cyberterrorism does not exist and is really a matter of hacking or information warfare. Those who hold this view disagree with labelling it 'terrorism' because it is unlikely that these acts cause fear, significant physical harm, or death.

How Serious Is the Problem of Cyberterrorism?

Ask Estonia [a country in the Baltic region of northern Europe]. The three-week cyber attack on Estonia threatened to black out the country's digital infrastructure, infiltrating the websites of the nation's banks and political institutions. What really keeps cybersecurity professionals up at night is not necessarily the threat of shutting down banking and financial infrastructures, rather the concern for the security of supervisory control and data acquisition (SCADA) systems related to the nation's critical infrastructures.

These are the industrial controls systems that are managed by computer systems. SCADA systems include railroad track switches, draw bridges, sewage treatment and water purification plants, traffic signals in busy cities, the electrical distribution grid, subway control systems, and other critical systems that can easily cause massive injuries and loss of life if exploited maliciously.

Many of these systems are connected to the Internet and run on commonly understood operating systems using well-known, standard communications protocols. In many cases, access to these systems is not controlled as tightly as expected given their potential impact on life and safety.

A concerted, focussed cyberterrorism attack on these systems could have a devastating effect on public safety and confidence. If terrorists were to attack a SCADA system simultaneously with physical bombings, public panic could quickly spin out of control. If terrorists were to bomb a busy city intersection while simultaneously shutting down the electrical systems in a nearby hospital—a combined attack known as a 'force multiplier' in military terms—this would result in national panic. The impact would be devastating to the surrounding population.

Some recent occurrences of cyberterrorism attacks on these systems include an incident in Romania where a cyberterrorist illegally gained access to the computers controlling the life support systems at an Antarctic research station, endangering the 58 scientists involved. Fortunately, the culprits were stopped before damage occurred.

Most acts of sabotage, while not politically motivated, have caused financial and other damage, as was the case where a disgruntled employee in Shire of Maroochy, Australia, caused the release of untreated sewage into water.

If Hollywood and popular fiction resemble future predictions, we might consider how cyberterrorism is being depicted in fictitious scenarios such as in Dan Brown's novel *Digital Fortress*, Amy Eastlake's *Private Lies*, and the Tom Clancy series Net Force (about an FBI/military team dedicated to combating cyberterrorists).

The films *Live Free or Die Hard* (a group of cyberterrorists intent on shutting down the entire computer network of the United States) or *Eagle Eye* (involving a supercomputer controlling everything electrical and networked to accomplish the goal), and a television episode of *24* which included plans to breach the nation's nuclear plant grid and then to seize control of the entire critical infrastructure protocol, are also examples of how media depicts cyberterrorism.

What Can We Do About Cyberterrorism?

The good news is that there are many highly trained, internationally certified, experienced security professionals thinking about this problem. They are participating in exercises, examining case studies, war-gaming various scenarios, and implementing solutions. These experts from military, industry, and academia work well together and offer a global perspective.

There is also an abundance of policies, practices, tests, hardware, software, literature, training and education designed to protect against cyber attacks, regardless of the source (terrorist or otherwise), to detect it immediately when it happens, and to respond to it quickly and effectively.

The threat of cyberterrorism, however, is similar to the threats of other types of network exploitation, and carries with it warnings. Firstly, while cyber defenders must confront the full range of security vulnerabilities, the cyberterrorists need to succeed in finding and exploiting only a single vulnerability to accomplish their mission. Therefore, the level of effort is significant for the defenders.

Secondly, terrorists are typically passionate about accomplishing their goals and are often willing to lose their own lives to accomplish massive destruction. However, while many security experts are professionals who take their work very seriously, they are generally not fanatics working 20 hours a day for an extreme ideology.

The third problem is that the Internet was not initially designed for confidentiality or integrity (two of the services of security). It was designed for availability and resiliency by providing a packet-switched network with alternate paths meshed together. The security services of confidentiality and integrity usually must be implemented at the application and end-point levels (computer, mobile phone, personal digital assistant, etc.).

While we may be somewhat positioned to defend against such acts, we must act now—as a government and as individuals—to fully meet the challenge of cyberterrorism. Some methods we may use include:

1. Implementing strong access control systems to ensure that only authorised individuals can access cyber systems

2. Using strong encryption to ensure confidentiality and integrity of information stored, processed, and transmitted on and through cyberspace

3. Closely monitoring all cyber activity by using log files and log analysers

4. Keeping policies up to date, and ensuring they are strictly enforced

5. Implementing effective detection systems to recognise cyber attacks quickly

6. Appointing active cybersecurity leadership to implement a real-time national defence strategy

Using Technology to Spread the Terrorist Ideology

IT [information technology] allows terrorist groups to spread their ideology and facilitates recruitment: In cyberspace (including the World Wide Web, intranets and extranets, as well as non-Internet sensitive networks), experts now talk of a "virtual caliphate" of some 4,000 pro–al Qaeda websites, blogs, chat rooms disseminating jihadist messages or propaganda. It is used for training, recruitment, disseminating tactics, techniques, procedures, financing (through Internet pay sites), or garnering support. It shows videos of executions of hostages or successful strikes. It contributes to the radicalization of young Muslims. Governments, not only in Western countries, are faced with the dilemma: how to reconcile freedom of speech with some control of means of communication that can be abused to promote violence, racial hatred or religious intolerance.

Marc Finaud, "Information Technology, Terrorism, and Global Security," GCSP Policy Brief, no. 1, June 19, 2006.

The Future of Cyberterrorism

A critical factor in defending against cyberterrorism is thinking towards the future. It is easy to fall into the trap of projecting what terrorists might do in the future to our current technologies. But, we must think about what terrorists might do in the future to our future technologies. This becomes doubly challenging since predicting the future is always difficult and this challenges us to predict the future in two dimensions. Future terrorists will not attack what we have now.

They will attack what we will have in the future. For example, as we evolve more towards virtual worlds, diskless workstations ('thin client'), and cloud computing, computing capabilities are being deployed at a national-level utility rather than as individual or corporate data systems. We would be wise to extrapolate into the future based on current trends, then to think about how cyberterrorists might attack our future environment and technology infrastructure.

In his best-selling book *The Big Switch*, Nicholas Carr compares current computer trends to those of electricity development. More than 100 years ago, individual factories built their own electrical generators using water wheels by the sides of rivers to generate their own personal electricity. As the electrical grid developed, it became more economical and efficient to produce electricity in massive central locations and to distribute the electricity to customers as a utility. This freed up corporations to focus on their core missions, without the encumbrance of managing their own electrical generating plant.

Similarly, software, hardware, and data may be provided as a central utility, supplying customers at low cost. This would liberate individuals and corporations to focus on their core missions, rather than maintaining an information technology department, dealing with security, applying updates and patches, managing a 'help desk', etc.

With our nation's cyber landscape destined to change, and cyberterrorism evolving its target of attack, we must channel our thoughts and actions towards the future of both cyberterrorism and technology; we must understand their convergence, and we must address the security requirements of that future.

Regardless of whether cyberterrorism is a misnomer; a serious threat to life, safety, and our critical infrastructures; or just an annoyance, we need to be ever vigilant and forward thinking to meet future challenges regarding cybersecurity.

│ *"No act of cyberterrorism has ever yet occurred and is unlikely to at any time in the future."*

The Threat of Cyberterrorism Is Exaggerated

Maura Conway

Although the threat of cyberterrorism is a popular media theme, cyberterrorism is actually highly unlikely, argues Maura Conway in the following viewpoint. Most terrorists do not have the technological knowledge to carry out a cyber attack, she asserts. Moreover, Conway maintains, cyber attacks, especially those that appear to be anonymous, do not create the spectacular visual images and publicity that terrorists crave. Nevertheless, she claims, fear of the unknown—technology and terrorism—leads some to conclude that cyberterrorism is a serious threat. Conway, whose research focuses on terrorism and the Internet, lectures on international security in the School of Law and Government at Dublin City University in Ireland.

As you read, consider the following questions:

1. In what way does Conway's view of cyberterrorism differ from that of FBI director Robert Mueller?

Maura Conway, "Viewpoint: Privacy and Security, Against Cyberterrorism," *Communications of the ACM*, vol. 54, no. 2, February 2011, pp. 26–28. Copyright © 2011 by Maura Conway. All rights reserved. Reproduced by permission.

2. In the author's view, into what broad categories can analyses of cyberterrorism be divided?

3. How does the author explain the persistent treatment of cyberterrorism on the part of journalists?

L ike the 2007 cyber attacks on Estonia,[1] the October 2010 Stuxnet botnet[2] attack on Iranian nuclear facilities made cyber-based attacks global news. The Estonian attacks were largely labeled a cyberwar by journalists, although some did invoke the concept of cyberterrorism. The Stuxnet attack, on the other hand, has been very widely described as cyberterrorism, including by the Iranian government.

Fueling Fears

Cyberterrorism is a concept that appears recurrently in contemporary media. It is not just reported upon in newspapers and on television, but is also the subject of movies (such as 1990's *Die Hard 2* and 2007's *Live Free or Die Hard*) and popular fiction books (for example, Winn Schwartau's 2002 novel *Pearl Harbor Dot Com*). This coverage is particularly interesting if one believes, as I do, that no act of cyberterrorism has ever yet occurred and is unlikely to at any time in the near future. Having said that, it is almost always portrayed in the press as either having already occurred or being just around the corner. As an academic, I'm not alone in arguing that no act of cyberterrorism has yet occurred and, indeed, some journalists agree; most, however, seem convinced as to the salience of this threat. Why?

1. Cyber attacks on Estonia began on April 27, 2007, and swamped websites of Estonian organizations, including Estonian parliament, banks, ministries, newspapers, and broadcasters. Responsibility for the attacks remains subject to dispute.
2. A botnet refers to a collection of compromised computers running programs such as worms, Trojan horses, or backdoors under a common command. A botnet's originator can control the group remotely and usually does so for nefarious purposes.

I can only surmise that, just as a large amount of social-psychological research has shown, the uncertain and the unknown generally produce fear and anxiety. This is the psychological basis of an effective movie thriller: The fear is greatest when you suspect something, but you're not certain what it is. The term "cyberterrorism" unites two significant modern fears: fear of technology and fear of terrorism. Fear of terrorism, though the likelihood of any one of us being the victim of terrorism is statistically insignificant, has become perhaps normalized; but fear of technology? In fact, for those unfamiliar with the workings of complex technologies, these are perceived as arcane, unknowable, abstract, and yet increasingly powerful and ubiquitous. Many people therefore fear that technology will become the master and humankind the servant. Couple this relatively new anxiety with age-old fears associated with apparently random violence and the result is a truly heightened state of alarm. Many journalists—although fewer technology journalists than others—have succumbed, like members of the general population, to these fears, to which the journalists have then added further fuel with their reporting.

The Definition Issue

The second stumbling block for journalists is that just as the definition of terrorism is fraught, so too is the definition of cyberterrorism. My preference is to distinguish between cyber-terrorism and terrorist use of the Net. This is the distinction FBI [Federal Bureau of Investigation] director Robert Mueller seemed implicitly to be drawing in a March 2010 speech in which he stated that "the Internet is not only used to plan and execute attacks; it is a target in and of itself. . . . We in the FBI, with our partners in the intelligence community, believe the cyberterrorism threat is real, and it is rapidly expanding." Where the FBI director and I diverge is in the efficacy of the cyberterrorist threat as opposed to that of everyday terrorist use of the Net (that is, for radicalization, researching and planning, financing, and other purposes).

Dorothy Denning's definitions of cyberterrorism are probably the most well known and respected. Her most recent attempt at defining cyberterrorism is: ". . .[H]ighly damaging computer-based attacks or threats of attack by non-state actors against information systems when conducted to intimidate or coerce governments or societies in pursuit of goals that are political or social. It is the convergence of terrorism with cyberspace, where cyberspace becomes the means of conducting the terrorist act. Rather than committing acts of violence against persons or physical property, the cyberterrorist commits acts of destruction or disruption against digital property."

Analyses of cyberterrorism can be divided into two broad categories on the basis of where the producers stand on the definition issue: those who agree broadly with Denning versus those who wish to incorporate . . . a host of other activities into the definition. The literature can also be divided on the basis of where the authors stand on the magnitude of the cyberterrorism threat. [Myriam] Dunn Cavelty uses the term "Hypers" to describe those who believe a cyberterrorist attack is not just likely, but imminent, and the term "De-Hypers" to describe those who believe such an attack is unlikely. Most journalists are hypers; on the other hand, I'm emphatically a de-hyper. In this [viewpoint], I lay out the three major reasons why.

Three Arguments Against Cyberterrorism

In my opinion, the three most compelling arguments against cyberterrorism are:

- The argument of Technological Complexity;

- The argument regarding 9/11 and the Image Factor; and

- The argument regarding 9/11 and the Accident Issue.

The first argument is treated in the academic literature; the second and third arguments are not, but ought to be. None of these are angles to which journalists appear to have devoted a lot of thought or given adequate consideration.

In the speech mentioned earlier, FBI director Mueller observed, "Terrorists have shown a clear interest in pursuing hacking skills. And they will either train their own recruits or hire outsiders, with an eye toward combining physical attacks with cyber attacks." That may very well be true, but the argument from Technological Complexity underlines that "wanting" to do something is quite different from having the ability to do the same. Here's why:

Violent jihadis' IT [information technology] knowledge is not superior. For example, in research carried out in 2007, it was found that of a random sampling of 404 members of violent Islamist groups, 196 (48.5%) had a higher education, with information about subject areas available for 178 individuals. Of these 178, some 8 (4.5%) had trained in computing, which means that out of the entire sample, less than 2% of the jihadis came from a computing background. And not even these few could be assumed to have mastery of the complex systems necessary to carry out a successful cyberterrorist attack.

Real-world attacks are difficult enough. What are often viewed as relatively unsophisticated real-world attacks undertaken by highly educated individuals are routinely unsuccessful. One only has to consider the failed car bomb attacks planned and carried out by medical doctors in central London and at Glasgow airport in June 2007.

Hiring hackers would compromise operational security. The only remaining option is to retain "outsiders" to undertake such an attack. This is very operationally risky. It would force the terrorists to operate outside their own circles and thus leave them ripe for infiltration. Even if they successfully got in contact with "real" hackers, they would be in no position to gauge their competency accurately; they would simply have to trust. . . . This would be very risky.

A Need for Terrifying Images

So on the basis of technical know-how alone, cyberterror attack is not imminent, but this is not the only factor one must take into account. The events of Sept. 11, 2001 [also known as 9/11; referring to the terrorist attacks on the United States], underscore that for a true terrorist event, spectacular, moving images are crucial. The attacks on the World Trade Center were a fantastic piece of performance violence; look back on any recent roundup of the decade and mention of 9/11 will not just be prominent, but pictures will always be provided.

The problem with respect to cyberterrorism is that many of the attack scenarios put forward, from shutting down the electric power grid to contaminating a major water supply, fail on this account: They are unlikely to have easily captured, spectacular (live, moving) images associated with them, something we—as an audience—have been primed for by the attack on the World Trade Center on 9/11.

The only cyberterrorism scenario that would fall into this category is interfering with air traffic control systems to crash planes, but haven't we seen that planes can much more easily be employed in spectacular "real-world" terrorism? And besides, aren't all the infrastructures just mentioned much easier and more spectacular to simply blow up? It doesn't end there, however. For me, the third argument against cyberterrorism is perhaps the most compelling; yet it is very rarely mentioned.

In 2004, Howard Schmidt, former White House cybersecurity coordinator, remarked to the U.S. Senate Committee on the Judiciary regarding Nimda and Code Red[3] that "we to this day don't know the source of that. It could have very easily been a terrorist." This observation betrays a fundamental misunderstanding of the nature and purposes of terrorism, particularly its attention-getting and communicative functions.

A terrorist attack with the potential to be hidden, portrayed as an accident, or otherwise remain unknown is unlikely to be viewed positively by any terrorist group. In fact, one of the most important aspects of the 9/11 attacks in New York from the perpetrators' viewpoint was surely the fact that while the first plane to crash into the World Trade Center could have been accidental, the appearance of the second plane confirmed the incident as a terrorist attack in real time. Moreover, the crash of the first plane ensured a large audience for the second plane as it hit the second tower.

Alternatively, think about the massive electric failure that took place in the northeastern U.S. in August 2003: If it was a terrorist attack—and I'm not suggesting that it was—but *if it was*, it would have been a spectacular failure.

The Costs Outweigh the Benefits

Given the high cost—not just in terms of money, but also time, commitment, and effort—and the high possibility of

---

3. Nimda, a quick-spreading computer worm and file infector, was released on September 18, 2001, and at the time eclipsed previous economic damage. Code Red was a July 13, 2001, computer worm that defaced websites with the phrase, "Hacked by Chinese!"

failure on the basis of manpower issues, timing, and complexity of a potential cyberterrorist attack, the costs appear to me to still very largely outweigh the potential publicity benefits. The publicity aspect is crucial for potential perpetrators of terrorism and so the possibility that an attack may be apprehended or portrayed as an accident, which would be highly likely with regard to cyberterrorism, is detrimental. Add the lack of spectacular moving images and it is my belief that cyberterrorism, regardless of what you may read in newspapers, see on television, or obtain via other media sources, is not in our near future.

So why then the persistent treatment of cyberterrorism on the part of journalists? Well, in this instance, science fiction–type fears appear to trump rational calculation almost every time.

"*Because of music piracy, the U.S. economy loses a total of $12.5 billion in economic output each year.*"

Music Piracy Poses a Serious Threat to the US Economy

Stephen E. Siwek

In the following viewpoint, economist Stephen E. Siwek asserts that the true cost of music piracy is not limited to lost product sales. In fact, he maintains, according to economic principles, changes in demand in one industry affect demand in others. Determining the actual economic cost of music piracy in the United States must therefore include losses in these interdependent industries, Siwek claims. Thus, he reasons, the true cost of music piracy when considering these "multiplying" economic factors is $12.5 billion—a significant loss. Lost tax dollars make the true cost even greater, he concludes. Siwek is an economic consultant whose focus is intellectual property industries.

As you read, consider the following questions:

1. According to the North American Industry Classification System, in what are 5122 industries primarily engaged?

2. According to Siwek, what estimated loss figure did the $5.333 billion music piracy loss in 2005 convert to when adding industry multipliers?

3. In the author's opinion, how much did sound recording piracy cost governments at all levels annually?

Widespread piracy of copyright-protected works through both physical and electronic media harms the companies that create and sell these products. Since many of these companies are U.S. firms, the harm of global piracy falls disproportionately on U.S. companies, their stockholders and employees, and on U.S. federal and state governments.

Studying the Economics of Intellectual Property

The U.S. companies that are most directly affected by piracy have long sought to increase understanding of the scope of this problem and to encourage government-wide efforts to address this threat. However, until recently, there has been little reliable economic information available to U.S. policy makers to assist them in balancing the importance of enforcing intellectual property rights as against other priorities. In order to address this issue, in 2005, I published a study, entitled "Engines of Growth: Economic Contributions of the U.S. Intellectual Property Industries." In that study, I analyzed the contributions to the U.S. economy of the U.S. "IP [intellectual property] industries"—industries that rely most heavily on copyright or patent protection to generate revenue, employ and compensate workers and contribute to real growth. The study found, among other things, that these IP industries are the most important growth drivers in the U.S. economy, contributing nearly 40% of the growth achieved by all U.S. private industry and nearly 60% of the growth of U.S. exportable products. It also found that the IP industries were responsible for one-fifth of the total U.S. private industry's contribution to GDP [gross domestic product] and two-fifths of the contribution of U.S. exportable products and services to GDP.

Subsequently, in September 2006, the Institute for Policy Innovation (IPI) published my new study, entitled "The True Cost of Motion Picture Piracy to the U.S. Economy." In that study (hereinafter, the "Motion Picture Piracy" study), I measured the true cost of motion picture piracy to the U.S. economy as a whole. I concluded that global piracy of motion pictures resulted in $20.5 billion annually in lost output among all U.S. industries, $5.5 billion annually in lost earnings for all U.S. workers and 141,030 U.S. jobs that would otherwise have been created. In addition, as a result of piracy, governments at the federal, state and local levels are deprived of at least $857 million in tax revenue each year.

The "Motion Picture Piracy" study was an initial effort to measure the economic impact of motion picture piracy on the U.S. economy as a whole.

In the current study, the basic methodology and approach that was pioneered in the "Motion Picture Piracy" study will be applied to another industry—the U.S. sound recording industry. In this analysis, as in the motion picture study, estimates of sound recording industry losses to piracy will be used in conjunction with industry-specific multipliers[1] from the U.S. Bureau of Economic Analysis to derive economy-wide losses in output, employee earnings and jobs. In addition, these estimates, in conjunction with other data, will be used to derive estimates of the tax receipts that are lost as a result of sound recording piracy. . . .

The U.S. Sound Recording Industries

In this study, the principal focus of analysis will be the U.S. sound recording industries that are identified in the North American Industry Classification System [NAICS] as a four-

---

1. A multiplier is an effect in economics in which an increase in spending produces an increase in national income and consumption greater than the initial amount spent.

digit industry group—NAICS 5122. This industry group "comprises establishments primarily engaged in

- producing and distributing musical recordings,

- in publishing music,

- or in providing sound recording and related services."

NAICS 5122 is part of the broader motion picture and sound recording industry subsector (NAICS 512) which is, in turn, part of the "information" industry sector (NAICS 51).

According to the U.S. Census Bureau, the "employer firms" in NAICS 5122 generated revenue of $18.7 billion in 2005. This total represented an increase of $2.2 billion or 13.7% over 2004. In that year (2004), the Census Bureau also found that the sound recording industries had 25,101 paid employees in 3,405 establishments. These employees received a total payroll of $1.965 billion.

Within the four-digit sound recording industries group, the largest five-digit NAICS industry is NAICS 51222—integrated record production and distribution. In 2005, the NAICS 51222 industry reported revenues of $12.866 billion. Of this total, 87 percent or $11.242 billion was generated through the sale of recordings. In 2005, the NAICS 51222 industry reported total expenses of $11.122 billion. This total represented an increase of 24.6% or $2.194 billion over total expenses in 2004. Personnel costs alone rose from $1.631 billion in 2004 to $2.173 billion in 2005.

The full impact of sound recording piracy is not limited to the U.S. companies that create and sell copy-protected music products. In particular, U.S. retailers of compact discs [CDs] face reduced sales and lower profits as a result of pirate activities that occur in the United States. The International Federation of the Phonographic Industry (IFPI) has reported that in 2005, U.S. sales of recorded music generated record company "trade" revenues of $7.012 billion. At the retail level, however, these same sales of recorded music in the U.S. cost consumers $12.270 billion. Clearly, in the U.S., recorded music piracy hurts both producers and retailers of recorded music.

The Interlocking Economy

In fact, the impact of music piracy flows throughout the U.S. economy. Piracy in one segment of the economy can affect other industries because the economy is an "interlocking" system. Changes in supply or demand in one industry can and do affect supply and demand in other industries.

For example, assume that personal watercraft suddenly become very popular and shortages develop. In this situation, the price of personal watercraft will rise and so will the profits of the manufacturers. However, in order to continue to earn these higher profits, the manufacturers will have to make more personal watercraft. In the process, they will buy, among other things, more waterproof seats from seat manufacturers.

Of course, it doesn't stop there. In order to produce more seats, the seat manufacturers will have to buy more plastic and more padding. And the plastic and padding manufacturers will have to buy more of the particular materials that they need.

The cascade does not even end with the suppliers of personal watercraft manufacturers but continues downstream as well. The retail sellers of personal watercraft who buy from the manufacturers will also be able to earn more money by raising prices or by increasing volume. These kinds of interactions among industries are captured in input-output tables. Input-output tables measure the interrelationships that exist among different industries. With this information, one can estimate what impact a specific change in one industry will have on other industries.

What is true for personal watercraft is equally true for recorded music. If the revenue generated by making and selling recorded music increases (in this case, not by higher demand

The Impact of Piracy Throughout the Economy

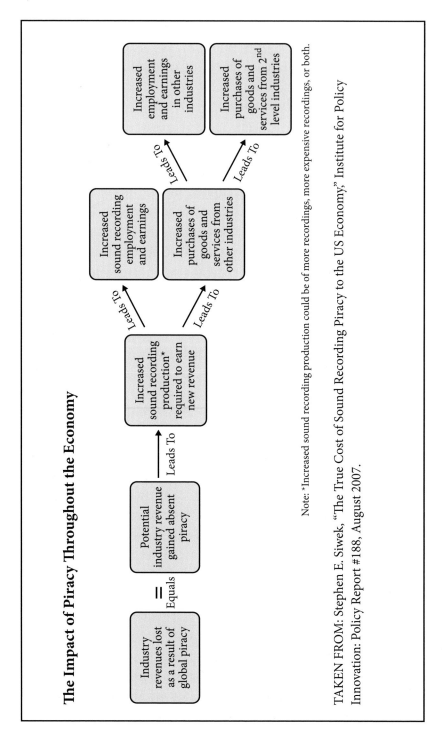

Note: *Increased sound recording production could be of more recordings, more expensive recordings, or both.

TAKEN FROM: Stephen E. Siwek, "The True Cost of Sound Recording Piracy to the US Economy," Institute for Policy Innovation: Policy Report #188, August 2007.

but by a decrease in piracy), record companies will make more recordings, invest in higher quality, broaden distribution or marketing, or some combination of these activities in order to capture more profits. . . .

Total Lost Output, Employment and Earnings

To produce industry-specific estimates of the impacts of piracy on the U.S. economy, the estimated losses from piracy for the sound recording industry are combined with the appropriate multipliers. . . .

As a result of piracy, the sound recording industries have sustained a reduction in final demand for their products in the amount of $5.333 billion in 2005. Using the relevant industry multipliers, this loss is converted into an estimate of the total loss in U.S. output. This total loss figure is $10.211 billion. In addition, the "direct" loss sustained by retailers of U.S. sound recordings ($1.04 billion) would provide an additional $2.290 billion in total lost output to the U.S. economy. As a result, the full impact of sound recording piracy on U.S. output was an overall loss of $12.501 billion.

With regard to lost earnings of U.S. workers, the comparable loss figures are $1.997 billion that stem from the losses sustained by the sound recording production and distribution industries and $699 million from the losses of retail sales of legitimate music CDs. Thus, the total loss in earnings to workers in 2005 was $2.697 billion.

Finally, in terms of losses in employment that would have been created, the effects of piracy on the sound recording industries in NAICS 5122 cost the United States 46,114 jobs and the effects on U.S. retail distribution cost 24,946 jobs. Thus, the total loss in U.S. employment that has resulted from piracy of U.S. sound recordings in 2005 was 71,060 jobs. . . .

We estimate that the direct loss in employee earnings in the U.S. sound recording and retail industries that results from pirate activities is $1.056 billion. The direct loss in employment at these industries was 26,860 jobs.

Lost Tax Revenues

In total, sound recording piracy costs government at all levels, conservatively $422 million annually. . . .

For the tax loss estimates presented in this study, the methodology previously used in the "Motion Picture Piracy" study was again applied to the sound recording industry.

As in the "Motion Picture Piracy" study, in this study, tax loss estimates are developed for three categories of taxes. These are lost personal income taxes that would have been paid by sound recording industry employees, lost corporate income taxes and lost production and other business taxes. . . . Personal income taxes would have exceeded $113 million from sound recording employees alone and more than $291 million from the total employees directly and indirectly affected by sound recording piracy. . . .

Focusing only on corporate income taxes, we estimate that the sound recording industry alone would have generated additional taxes of $81 million each year. In addition, lost "production" taxes from the U.S. sound recording industry would have exceeded $50 million annually.

It is important also to recognize that the tax loss estimates presented here do not encompass a full accounting of all tax losses attributable to piracy. The estimates for both corporate income tax losses and production tax losses reflect only the direct losses sustained by the sound recording industries themselves. The estimates do not include additional tax losses that would result from lower income and lower sales in those U.S. industries that supply inputs to the U.S. copyright industries. *Thus the corporate income tax and production tax estimates do not include tax losses sustained at U.S. industries that are indirectly affected by piracy.*

As set forth in this [viewpoint], the U.S. sound recording industries are now sustaining approximately $5.33 billion in losses as a result of global and U.S. piracy. In addition, U.S. retailers are losing another $1.04 billion. These estimates suggest total "direct" losses to all U.S. industries from music piracy that exceed $6.37 billion.

These direct losses then cascade through the rest of the U.S. economy, and the losses of economic output, jobs and employee earnings "multiply."

Based on the analyses set forth in this [viewpoint], because of music piracy, the U.S. economy loses a total of $12.5 billion in economic output each year.

Furthermore, the U.S. economy also loses 71,060 jobs. Of this amount, 46,114 jobs are lost at the U.S. production level for sound recordings while 24,946 jobs are lost at the U.S. retail level.

Because of global piracy in recorded music, U.S. employees lose $2.7 billion in total earnings annually. Of this total, $2.0 billion is lost at the U.S. production level while $700 million is lost at the U.S. retail level.

Finally, as a consequence of piracy in sound recordings, U.S. federal, state and local governments lose a minimum of $422 million in tax revenues annually. Of this amount, $291 million represents lost personal income taxes while $131 million is lost corporate income and production taxes.

> "Studies that overstate the economic ef-
> fect of piracy . . . obscure the fact that
> the music industry still has some seri-
> ous work to do on its business model."

The Economic Impact of Music Piracy Is Exaggerated

Eric Bangeman

*Claims that music piracy leads to billions in lost economic out-
put use flawed reasoning, claims Eric Bangeman in the following
viewpoint. The assumption that absent piracy, most illegal downloads would lead to sales is unsupported, he maintains. Moreover, Bangeman argues, some illegal file sharing actually leads to
sales. In fact, he asserts, other industry factors such as the transition from physical to digital media contribute more to lost sales
than piracy. Rather than focus on piracy, the music industry
should work on adjusting to the way the modern market con-
sumes music, he reasons. Bangeman is managing editor of Ars
Technica, a technology news and policy analysis website.*

As you read, consider the following questions:

1. According to Bangeman, what must the Institute for
   Policy Innovation (IPI) study do for readers to believe
   that 20 percent of illegally downloaded songs would
   have been purchased?

2. What assumption does the IPI study make about the music market, in the author's view?

3. In the author's opinion, what agenda does the IPI have a history of pushing?

A new study from the Institute for Policy Innovation [IPI] takes a different approach to quantifying the cost of music piracy. Instead of just focusing on what the lost sales cost the record labels, the new study measures the impact of piracy on the US economy. The total price tag? A cool $12.5 billion in lost output, if you trust the study's numbers.

Along with the multibillion-dollar loss, piracy also is hindering job growth, according to the IPI. The US economy will lose 71,060 jobs due to piracy, with almost 38 percent of those (26,860) in the recording industry. That amounts to $2.7 billion in lost earnings. Piracy also hits Uncle Sam—as well as state and local governments—right in the pocketbook, with at least $422 million in lost tax revenues.

Problematic Assumptions

The study makes for some alarming reading, but it suffers from a few significant flaws. First and foremost, it appears to fall into the "illicit downloads = lost sales" fallacy, the view that each song obtained over a P2P [peer-to-peer] network is a lost *purchase*. "Unfortunately, there is no precise measure of the degree to which consumers of pirated CDs [compact discs] would continue to purchase those CDs at legitimate prices," according to the study. "While the degree to which these legitimate purchases would occur differs by market, it appears nevertheless that such purchases would comprise a very significant fraction of the total number of pirated CDs now purchased. . . . In this study, the weighted average substitution rate used for the physical piracy of recorded music is 65.7 percent. It is then assumed that only 20% (1 in 5) of these downloaded songs would have been purchased legitimately if piracy did not exist."

That's a bit better than the one-to-one argument, but not by much. It essentially assumes that one of every five downloaded songs *would* have been purchased, were it not for file sharing [the practice of distributing or providing access to digitally stored information such as computer programs, multimedia, or electronic books]. Although a 20 percent figure may not look like much, it is still a percentage not justified by our own knowledge of file-sharing trends. The study needs to make a firm argument for why this percentage is so high. It's a flaw similar to that in a 2006 study commissioned by the MPAA [Motion Picture Association of America].

Note that the assumption cuts both ways. Not only does it assume many would-be sales, but it also ignores sales that do stem from file sharing. P2P users buy a lot of music, after all. Three out of four P2P users said that they bought music after downloading it online, with 21 percent of the respondents to the survey, commissioned by the Canadian Recording Industry Association, saying that they have bought previously downloaded music on more than 10 occasions. So here again, we have data which would necessarily lower the study's estimates not being taken into account.

Another study even goes so far as to argue that the effect of file sharing on legal music sales is "not statistically distinguishable from zero." Published this past February [2007] in the *Journal of Political Economy*, the study tracked the effects of 1.75 million song downloads on 680 albums. The researchers concluded that the availability—and even increased downloads—of music on P2P networks did not correlate to a negative effect on music sales. "Even our most negative point estimate implies that a one-standard-deviation increase in file sharing reduces an album's weekly sales by a mere 368 copies, an effect that is too small to be statistically distinguishable from zero," the study's authors reported.

The Digital Marketplace

The IPI study also assesses the increased demand for music if piracy didn't exist and assumes the market would remain as "intensely competitive" as it is today. The problem is that music fans are largely disenchanted with the market. By and large, music fans think that music is too expensive and that much of what is available isn't very good. 58 percent of those responding to a study commissioned by *Rolling Stone* magazine and the Associated Press said that music is declining in quality. And although the DRM [digital rights management; anti-piracy technology] situation is looking up these days, it can still be a confusing morass with unanticipated side effects for consumers, as the recently announced closure of the Google video store demonstrates.

Consumer apathy aside, there are other factors at work in the music industry. One of the biggest is the transition from sales of physical media to digital media. CD sales have dropped sharply since the beginning of the decade, and projections indicate that there's no end in sight to the decline. Sure, downloads have picked up since 2004, but not at a rate that will come close to overcoming the slide in CD sales. The individual song download angle is largely ignored by the IPI's study as well, which is fixated on sales of physical media.

A Pro-Market Agenda

The IPI has a history of pushing what it calls a pro-market agenda with its research, including one study asking if open source [a philosophy that promotes free redistribution and access to software design and implementation details] has reached its limits and another similar to that under discussion here that attempts to quantify the economic impact of movie piracy. Given its track record (which includes this gem from the aforementioned open-source study: "Open source will go the way of other IT [information technology] industry fads that were once trumpeted as the way of the future . . .") and ideological bent, the results of this study are rather unsurprising.

When the discussion over dollar figures and economic impact comes to an end, most people will agree that file sharing is a real issue for the recording industry and that there is a financial cost that goes along with it. It's also true that piracy has something of a ripple effect, reaching beyond the artists and record labels. But studies that overstate the economic effect of piracy do little to further the discussion over issues of copyright, file sharing, and DRM, and they obscure the fact that the music industry still has some serious work to do on its business model.

Periodical and Internet Sources Bibliography

The following articles have been selected to supplement the diverse views presented in this chapter.

Tal Be'ery	"New Tool Enables the Automation of Social Engineering Attacks on Facebook," *Software World*, November 2011.
Congressional Digest	"History of the Internet Piracy Debate," November 2011.
Eamonn Forde	"Artists: Embrace Progress and Prosper," *Music Week*, February 6, 2010.
David Gewirtz	"State Sponsored Cyberterrorism," *Journal of Counterterrorism & Homeland Security International*, vol. 16, no. 1, 2010.
Misha Glenny	"The Cyber Arms Race Has Begun," *Nation*, October 31, 2011.
Patrick Marshall	"Cybersecurity," *CQ Researcher*, February 26, 2010.
David M. Nicol	"Hacking the Lights Out: The Computer Virus Threat to the Electrical Grid," *Scientific American*, July 2011.
Divyadarshini Patel	"Virtual Felony," *Skills Ahead*, September 1, 2010. www.mediamates.biz/skills_ahead.
Bill Roth	"Focus on Cyber-Crime Misses the Real Emerging Threat," *Software World*, July 2010.
Steven Seidenberg	"The Record Business Blues," *ABA Journal*, June 2010.
Stephen M. Walt	"Is the Cyber Threat Overblown?," *Foreign Policy*, March 30, 2010.

OPPOSING
VIEWPOINTS®
SERIES

CHAPTER 2

How Do Cybercriminals Use Online Media to Commit Crimes?

Chapter Preface

"Staying indoors is no longer the best way to avoid bumping into people you don't want to see," claims the British Computer Society (BCS), an information technology think tank. In fact, the BCS concludes, "Given the ubiquitous presences of technology, your own kitchen, study or bedroom can become the place where harassers can reach you most easily." The challenge for legal scholars is whether those using online technologies to harass others are communicating publicly or privately. Cyber stalking—the use of the Internet to harass, stalk, or threaten a victim—is a crime. If the online harassment is considered a public communication, then it is protected political speech. If the online harassment is considered a private, personal communication, it would be cyber stalking. Indeed, one of the controversies in the debate surrounding the criminal use of emerging online media is whether online communications are public or private.

In August 2011, the Federal Bureau of Investigation (FBI) filed a cyber stalking complaint against William Lawrence Cassidy, who had published eight thousand threatening and harassing Twitter posts about Buddhist leader Alyce Zeoli. Cassidy had joined Zeoli's organization, Kunzang Palyul Choling (KPC), in 2007. However, when it was discovered that he had used a false name and fabricated his claim to have lung cancer, the relationship disintegrated, and Cassidy began his barrage of threatening Twitter posts. Attorney Shanlon Wu, who represents Zeoli, claims that Zeoli "felt constantly attacked and monitored by these anonymous people, and the attacks went on whether or not she was online." The FBI claims that Cassidy's relentless tweets caused Zeoli substantial emotional distress that made her fear for her life. In fact, at the time of the complaint, she had not left her house for one and a half years.

In December 2011, however, federal district court judge Roger W. Titus dismissed the indictment, arguing that the First Amendment protects anonymous speech. In his opinion, he concludes that "Twitter and blogs are today's equivalent of a bulletin board that one is free to disregard, in contrast, for example, to e-mails or phone calls directed to a victim." Titus reasoned that people choose to read a blog or follow Twitter just as people choose to look at a bulletin board. The free speech advocacy group the Electronic Frontier Foundation agrees, adding, "While not all speech is protected by the First Amendment, the idea that the courts must police every inflammatory word spoken online not only chills freedom of speech but is unsupported by decades of First Amendment jurisprudence."

Some legal analysts dispute these claims. According to Julie Hilden, a lawyer who writes on First Amendment issues, the bulletin board analogy is not quite fair to harassment victims. Electronic forums like Twitter are not as fixed as a bulletin board, where one chooses whether to walk up and read its contents, she maintains. "If you have a practice, as many people do, of searching your name every so often," Hilden explains, "then you may inevitably encounter negative posting that you'd rather not have read, and that may even be harassing toward you."

Whether harassing content on electronic media is criminal cyber stalking or protected speech remains controversial. The authors in the following chapter present their views on how individuals use online media to commit crimes. How the law will be applied to the use of ever-evolving online technologies will remain a challenge. Indeed, according to Santa Clara University law professor Eric Goldman, "you have to figure out if old law maps to new interactions."

> "If the [sextortion] victim is too fright-
> ened to put a stop to it, the requests
> sometimes become so provocative, they
> develop into hard-core pornography."

Fighting Back
Online Predators

Kim Hone-McMahan

In the following viewpoint, Akron (OH) Beacon Journal staff writer Kim Hone-McMahan tells the story of Ashley, a victim of online "sextortion," a crime in which predators blackmail victims into providing increasingly explicit sexual images. Some online predators pose as professional photographers who encourage victims, mostly teens, to post provocative photos, and when victims refuse to provide more explicit pictures, the predators threaten to post the original photos for others to see, the author claims. Law enforcement officers struggle to catch these predators because embarrassment and fear of being charged with child pornography discourage victims from reporting the crime, Hone-McMahan maintains. Ashley encourages victims to report this crime despite their fears, to prevent predators from hurting others.

As you read, consider the following questions:

1. What happened when Ashley blocked an online predator from finding her on the Internet?

2. According to Mark Moretti of the office of the Ohio attorney general, why do offenders get away with sextortion?

3. How did Ashley's social network behavior change after her experience?

Ashley knew there were adults on the Internet who preyed on kids, especially pretty girls like her. She had watched reruns of the television show *To Catch a Predator*. But she thought she was smarter than the girls who fell for online perverts. That was right up until the day she got a message demanding that she strip down in front of her webcam—or else.

"If you get naked all da way, I'll never bother u again," the guy said during a live chat session with Ashley on Stickam, a social network.

If she refused, the predator promised, he would post a topless video of her online for her mom, friends and all the world to see. He had taken the video without her knowledge.

It's called sextortion, a form of blackmail. If the victim is too frightened to put a stop to it, the requests sometimes become so provocative, they develop into hard-core pornography. And because of the ever-increasing use of computers by children, the Ohio attorney general's office expects this type of misuse to increase.

"Hahahahah your a joke," she wrote back. "Go ahead and ruin my life. You do that, I'll kill myself and ull go to jail for the rest of your life. They will find you."

Ashley, whose name has been changed to protect her from the predator, routinely used chat sites to talk with people she met on the Internet. It was on Stickam that the man first contacted her last August, engaging her in small talk. Within a few days, he offered to make the 16-year-old a model.

Like most teenagers, she was flattered. Tall, thin and beautiful, she had heard the suggestion from others, so the proposition didn't seem implausible.

The man said if it was decided that she was good model material, he would pay for her to go to Myrtle Beach for a swimwear shoot on Labor Day. She asked whether her mom could tag along.

"You're under 18, a parent would have to come with you," he said.

That made Ashley feel better about what seemed too good to be true. Sounding knowledgeable about the modeling industry, he convinced her to pose partially nude on Skype, a software application that allows people to talk and see each other through the Internet. But while he was able to see her, he blocked his own image from her view.

Alarmed by his push for her to strip completely so he could determine whether she had the figure to be a model, she hurriedly ended the session—but not before she asked whether he had a website.

"Still don't believe I'm legit?" he asked, not offering any additional information.

"Idk [I don't know]. I'm not sure," she replied.

Embarrassed by what had taken place, she blocked the man from finding her on the Internet, or so she thought. Ten days later, he appeared again, pretending to be a different person, and instructed her to visit a photographer's website to see his work. He then urged her to get in front of the camera wearing only underwear so that he could judge whether she would be a good fit for a photo shoot taking place in Dublin, Ohio.

"Pretty standard stuff," he told her.

This time, though, she quickly put a stop to it, telling him that she didn't trust him and charging that he was both a pervert and pedophile.

Then the blackmail began.

He said that he had secretly recorded the earlier session, when she had stripped to just a bikini bottom. And if she didn't do what he wanted, he would post it for all to see.

To make it stop, she agreed to send him two partially nude pictures of herself. But it wasn't enough. He continued to stalk her and demanded she pose nude in another video. If she agreed, the man said, he would end the threats.

"What you are doing is a crime," she said. "I'm telling . . ."

Ashley worried that her mother would think badly of her, but Mom realized her daughter had been tricked by someone who preys on children and called the police.

Akron juvenile police detectives haven't heard much yet about sextortion by strangers. Instead, they generally see cases of teenage girls who take nude pictures of themselves, send them to a boyfriend and after a breakup, the jilted lover shares the photos with pals. There are probably many incidents involving nude photos online that go unreported because of the embarrassment factor.

Detective Mary Braun of the Cincinnati police, who specializes in computer investigations involving things like sextortion and child pornography, said her department has had calls from departments across the country seeking advice. As part of the Regional Electronic Computer Intelligence Task Force, a joint effort by Cincinnati and Hamilton County, Braun maintains that victims need to be brave enough to report the crime so police can catch the blackmailer.

"It's normal to feel embarrassed. But remember, you are the victim, not the offender," said Mark Moretti, public information officer for the office of Ohio Attorney General Mike DeWine. "You are not alone. Others have been through the

"Grooming" Victims

Those [Internet predators] seeking face-to-face meetings create bogus identities online, sometimes posing as teenagers. Then they troll the Internet for easy victims—youngsters with low self-esteem, problems with their parents, or a shortage of money. The pedophile might find a 14-year-old girl, for example, who has posted seemingly harmless information on her space for anyone to see. The pedophile sends a message saying he goes to high school in a nearby town and likes the same music or TV shows she likes.

Then the pedophile cultivates a friendly online relationship that investigators call "grooming." It could continue for days or weeks before the pedophile begins bringing up sexual topics, asking for explicit pictures or for a personal meeting. By that time an emotional connection has been made—and pedophiles can be master manipulators. Even if an actual meeting never takes place, it is important to note that youngsters can be victimized by such sexually explicit online contact.

Federal Bureau of Investigation,
"Child Predators: The Online Threat Continues to Grow,"
May 17, 2011. www.fbi.gov.

same situation as you are going through. Offenders get away with this type of behavior because they count on their victims not reporting it."

Ashley and her mom filed a police report but became nervous when an officer explained that, technically, Ashley could be charged with a felony. Akron Police Sgt. Brian Harding said that while he doesn't particularly like the Ohio law as it pertains to juveniles, it's possible that for distributing nude photos of themselves or someone else, they could face charges, such as delinquency by means of illegal use of a minor in nudity-oriented materials.

Worried that she could get in trouble with the law, potentially hurting her chances at scholarships, college admission and a job in the medical field, Ashley shied away from involving the police any further.

"I have to tell parents that by the sheer reading of the [Ohio] Revised Code, their teenager is guilty of creating child pornography. I would be remiss if I didn't tell them. However, in a fact pattern like this, I would not charge a juvenile with a felony," said Harding, agreeing with Braun that it's imperative for people to report claims of sextortion to authorities.

Federal prosecutors warn that sextortion crimes are on the rise. In Wisconsin, an 18-year-old received 15 years in prison after tricking his classmates into sending nude photos of themselves and then extorting them for sex. In Alabama, a 24-year-old man was sentenced to 18 years in prison for extorting nude pictures from women in three states. And in California, the FBI arrested a man in November after an investigation found that he had extorted more than 200 people, including more than three dozen juveniles.

As for the man extorting Ashley, police have transcripts of the discussion between the pair and are continuing their search. Chances are, Braun said, she's not the only teenager he has been threatening.

Ashley wasn't looking for a story to be written about herself. Instead, she responded to a request by the *Beacon Journal* for suggestions for the kinds of stories that reporters should write that affect teenagers. Longing to warn others, she suggested a story about sextortion.

"Teenagers are easily manipulated, . . ." she wrote in her e-mail to the paper. "People . . . don't realize that this is a real issue that happens to teenagers all of the time. I am not afraid to admit that I have been a victim of this [sextortion]. It is very scary and not something I would want to ever go through again."

Though Ashley called herself dumb for falling victim to the pedophile, she's far from it—carrying a 4-point average in high school.

"Even smart kids can be naive," her mother said while sitting in the living room of their Summit County home.

Ashley said she automatically used to add anyone, known or not, to her Facebook account. The practice allowed strangers to view private information, including photos. Now, she is more careful, and she's adamant about wanting others to be selective when deciding whom to add as friends on social networks.

She also urges those who are victims of sextortion to tell their parents and police—even if they are ashamed. Not doing so gives the predator license to continue making a girl or boy's life a living hell.

"Chances are my guy's probably out there blackmailing another girl," Ashley lamented. "And the extortion will go on, and on, and on because she's too afraid of what will happen if she tries to make it stop."

"While online solicitation of children by adult strangers does exist, it is a much smaller threat than [some] have claimed."

The Number of Predators That Exploit Children Online Is Exaggerated

Steve Rendall

Research shows no evidence that online predators are a serious threat to America's children, argues Steve Rendall in the following viewpoint. Indeed, children are at greater risk from online harassment by their peers, he claims. Nevertheless, Rendall asserts, television networks continue to exploit unwarranted fears. Television programs such as To Catch a Predator *create rather than report news, and by pandering to sensationalism, they suffer from questionable journalistic ethics, he maintains. Such efforts to exploit unsubstantiated fears for profit have created an unnecessary moral panic, he concludes. Rendall, a researcher at Fairness & Accuracy in Reporting (FAIR), hosts the organization's radio show,* CounterSpin.

As you read, consider the following questions:

1. Who does Rendall claim are some of the biggest beneficiaries of the online predator scare?

2. According to the author, what finally motivated NBC to cancel production of *To Catch a Predator*?

3. How many examples of a minor who met an adult for sexual purposes as a result of online activities did the Crimes Against Children Research Center survey find?

There is money to be made from fear—and business has been good for those hawking the online child predator threat.

Exploiting Fear

Exploiters of the scare range from the Internet-policing groups who ferret out suspects and share information with authorities (and sometimes, for a fee, with journalists) to vendors of software intended to help parents monitor and restrict web use. Some of the biggest beneficiaries are TV companies that feature salacious segments on how predators stalk the web in hopes of arranging live liaisons with their young prey. Of course, it's all in the spirit of public service and protecting the children, right?

CNN says so: "It's a scary reality. Your children are vulnerable to predators online," remarked CNN's Gerri Willis (7/28/07), reporting on "the need to increase awareness of online predators."

And Bill O'Reilly (Fox News, 10/4/07) says it's a big problem, too: "Every day we're seeing kids molested, murdered, kidnapped because they are meeting people on the Net and then they go meet them in person. And that's just insane."

The threat has been the subject of any number of television newsmagazine segments (ABC's *Nightline*, 9/25/08; CBS's *Early Show*, 11/22/07), as well as the Fox broadcast network's *America's Most Wanted* (8/8/09, 1/3/09, 2/6/09).

But it's an NBC show that gets the top award for ceaseless flogging of the theme.

If you wanted to watch something besides football last Super Bowl Sunday, you could tune into MSNBC's "Predator Bowl"—12 hours of wall-to-wall episodes of NBC *Dateline*'s popular (if critically scorched) *To Catch a Predator*. The show features men who have talked dirty on the Internet with actors posing as minors. The men are lured by the actors to supposed live liaisons, where *Dateline* anchor Chris Hansen grills them about their motives and reads their smutty letters back to them—and, voyeuristically, to the viewers. Each episode ends with the subject being tackled by waiting police.

Questionable Journalistic Ethics

The show was always a mess from the point of journalism. It created news rather than reporting it; it surrendered its independence by working hand in glove with police agencies; and it paid sources. (NBC paid hundreds of thousands of dollars to the online policing group Perverted Justice for information and help in setting up stings.) Moreover, the show's week-in and week-out pounding on the same theme suggested it had less to do with journalism and public service than with pandering for ratings through salacious exploitation.

But appeals to journalism ethics left NBC News executives unmoved until one of the show's stings resulted in the suicide of a target: a former Texas prosecutor who had allegedly engaged in online sexual conversations with one of *Dateline*'s "minors." When the subject failed to show at the arranged rendezvous/sting, he was tracked by police and NBC to his home. As they arrived, he shot himself to death (*New York Times*, 6/26/08).

In addition to the suicide, for which NBC paid an out-of-court settlement, there were embarrassing reports that many of the "cases" in which *Dateline* had been involved had been thrown out of court, reportedly because NBC's and Perverted Justice's involvement interfered with proper police evidence-gathering procedures (*20/20*, 9/7/07; AP [Associated Press], 6/28/07).

This was finally enough to get NBC News to cancel production of the show in December 2008—but not quite enough to get them to stop airing it. Since its cancellation, *Predator* has lived on in perpetual reruns on NBC's cable outlet MSNBC, with the "Predator Bowl" merely the program's most prominent recent showcase.

To Catch a Predator might be dismissed as just a sleazy scramble for ratings, but its producers claim to be motivated by a genuine journalistic concern. *Predator* host Chris Hansen says the threat is "an epidemic" (*Dateline*, 12/23/06), that "the scope of the problem is immense" (MSNBC.com, 11/3/05) and it "seems to be getting worse" (*Dateline*, 12/16/05). On his MSNBC blog, the anchor claimed that "one in five children online is solicited for sex by an adult" (2/6/06) and "at any given time, 50,000 predators are on the Internet prowling for children" (11/3/05).

Examining the Research

This would all seem highly newsworthy, not to mention alarming. But the fact is that researchers reject these claims—and with them the show's journalistic premise.

According to a new report from Harvard University's Berkman Center for Internet & Society ("Enhancing Child Safety and Online Technologies," 12/31/08), while online solicitation of children by adult strangers does exist, it is a much smaller threat than Hansen and others have claimed.

The researchers, examining existing research, found that roughly 1 percent of minors were threatened by online advances from adult strangers, and that the small cohort that were most threatened had home situations such as drug abuse or absent or disengaged parents that put them at higher risk in all aspects of their lives, online and off. The Harvard study concluded that minors were under greater risk from online harassment and bullying by their peers than from adult sexual "predators."

Social Networking Sites Are Not Inherently Risky

When a medium becomes used by a huge portion of the population, . . . it inevitably becomes a venue for deviant activity by some, but it is not necessarily a risk promoter. . . . Studies are needed about specific activities and environments of young people that are associated with risk. But so far studies have not shown that simply using a social networking site is risky in the absence of other behaviors such as responding to sexual overtures made via such sites. The fact that some online predation involved the use of social networking sites may simply reflect the broad use of such sites as a communication and interaction tool in current society.

Janis Wolak, David Finkelhor, and Kimberly Mitchell,
"Trends in Arrests of 'Online Predators,'"
Crimes Against Children Research Center, March 31, 2009.

So where did Hansen and others (e.g., ABC News, 5/3/06; CNN.com, 4/20/06) get the claims that "one in five" minors have been sexually solicited by adults online, or that "50,000 predators" are trolling the Internet right now?

Distorting the Findings

In the first case, by distorting the findings of a 2000 study by the Crimes Against Children Research Center at the University of New Hampshire. That study, surveying 1,501 minor Internet users (aged 10 to 17), found that 19 percent of them reported "at least one instance of unwanted sex talk (from other teenagers), or sex talk from an adult (whether wanted or not), in the past year." Eighty-two percent of such contacts came from other minors, so the proportion of minors who had an online sexual episode with an adult was more like 1 in 30 than 1 in 5.

And the researchers were asking about contacts that fell short of actual sexual solicitation. What the researchers called "aggressive sexual solicitation" accounted for just 3 percent of overall contacts—but, since 66 percent of those approaches were by peers, the actual instance of minors who were aggressively sexually solicited by adults on the Internet was roughly 1 percent.

The survey did not turn up a single example of a minor who ended up meeting an adult for sexual purposes as a result of these online activities.

Harvard's 2008 study clarified the point further:

> Other peers and young adults account for 90 percent–94 percent of solicitations in which approximate age is known. Also, many acts of solicitation online are harassing or teasing communications that are not designed to seduce youth into off-line sexual encounters; 69 percent of solicitations involve no attempt at off-line contact. Misperception of these findings perpetuates myths that distract the public from solving the actual problems youth face.

Inventing Numbers

And the "50,000 predators" figure? In a thorough report on the predator scare and the media's role in it (9/06), *Skeptical Inquirer* magazine's Benjamin Radford explained how the NBC anchor more or less concocted the number, which had been repeated in influential circles:

> As it turns out, Attorney General [Alberto] Gonzales had taken his 50,000 Web predator statistic not from any government study or report, but from NBC's *Dateline* TV show. *Dateline*, in turn, had broadcast the number several times without checking its accuracy. In an interview on NPR's *On*

the Media program [5/26/06], Hansen admitted that he had no source for the statistic, and stated that "it was attributed to, you know, law enforcement, as an estimate, and it was talked about as sort of an extrapolated number."

Radford concluded that the predator scare fits the definition of a "moral panic," a sociological term "describing a social reaction to a false or exaggerated threat to social values by moral deviants." The evidence certainly suggests that the online child predator scare would fit comfortably alongside such other greatly exaggerated or concocted threats as the Salem witch trials, the Satanic ritual murder scare and the crack baby epidemic (*Extra!*, 9–10/98). But in this case, the panic is not just being driven by outrage over an alleged threat to the moral order, but by the profit motives of an industry directly exploiting the scare.

| *"Many active Facebook users take risks that can lead to burglaries, identity theft, and stalking."*

Cybercriminals Use Personal Information on Social Networking Websites to Commit Crimes

Consumer Reports

Cybercriminals use social networking sites such as Facebook to commit crimes, claim the editors of Consumer Reports *in the following viewpoint. People often share personal information on Facebook that criminals use to burglarize homes, steal identities, and stalk victims, the editors explain. Facebook, they warn, is not interested in protecting users but instead using them to make money from advertisers and application developers, a fact consumers often ignore. In fact, some policy makers believe that the privacy policies on social networking sites invite fraud and put vulnerable children at risk, the editors report.* Consumer Reports *publishes reviews and comparisons of products and services, as well as conducts surveys on issues affecting consumers.*

As you read, consider the following questions:

1. According to *Consumer Reports*, how many households experienced some type of abuse on Facebook in 2010?

2. How do some headhunters use social network data, in the editors' view?

3. In the editors' opinion, what prompted howls from several members of Congress?

More than 5 million online U.S. households experienced some type of abuse on Facebook in the past year [2010], including virus infections, identity theft, and for a million children, bullying, a *Consumer Reports* survey shows.

And consumers are at risk in myriad other ways, according to our national State of the Net survey of 2,089 online households conducted earlier this year [2011] by the Consumer Reports National Research Center. Here are the details:

- Overall, online threats continue at high levels. One-third of households we surveyed had experienced a malicious software infection in the previous year. All told, we estimate that malware cost consumers $2.3 billion last year and caused them to replace 1.3 million PCs [personal computers].

- Millions of people jeopardize bank information, medical records, and other sensitive data they store on mobile phones, we project. Almost 30 percent in our survey who said they use their phone in such ways didn't take precautions to secure their phones.

- Many active Facebook users take risks that can lead to burglaries, identity theft, and stalking. Fifteen percent had posted their current location or travel plans, 34 percent their full birth date, and 21 percent of those with children at home had posted those children's names and photos. Moreover, roughly one in five hadn't used Facebook's privacy controls, making them more vulnerable to threats.

- Twenty-three percent of active Facebook users didn't know some of their "friends" well enough to feel completely comfortable about their own or their family's security or safety. An additional 6 percent admitted to having a friend who made them uneasy about those things. That means almost one in three Facebook users aren't fully comfortable with all their friends.

- The persistence of Internet threats makes it important to use security software. In our tests, we found that free anti-malware programs should provide adequate protection for many people.

Facing Up to Facebook

If you're like some 150 million Americans, you share the details of your life on Facebook, assuming that you and other users are its main customers and that it's accountable to you. But Bruce Schneier, chief security technology officer at security firm BT Global Services, says you're not Facebook's customer. "You are Facebook's product that they sell to their customers," he says, referring to the network's advertisers.

With "Find us on Facebook" tags popping up in malls, on popular TV shows, and elsewhere, Facebook has a lot of product to sell. And with no comparable alternative service, consumers are left as fodder for Facebook's advertisers and app [application] developers. "You are on Facebook because everybody else is," Schneier says. "You can say 'I don't like Facebook, I'm going to LiveJournal,' and suddenly you're alone."

Its position as the king of social networks has made Facebook the custodian of arguably the nation's largest collection of details about consumers' personal lives. "Any time you have a party with such a large amount of data, there's reason for concern," says Justin Brookman, director of consumer privacy for the nonprofit Center for Democracy & Technology.

Access to Data by Outsiders

Already, use of that data by outsiders is widespread. It might not be news that people have been fired because they posted ill-considered status updates or photos. But job recruiters might check Facebook to find out who people are connected to.

One recruiter told us that headhunters have used social network data to make sure job candidates are a fit with their clients. So if you lost out on a job because of Facebook, it might not have been because of just one indiscretion. You might have been rejected because an employer or recruiter found telling details in your postings, even though such a rejection might constitute discrimination.

Facebook posts are also widely used as evidence in divorce and family-law cases. Randall Kessler of Kessler, Schwarz & Solomiany, chair-elect of the American Bar Association's family-law section, says he advises new clients to "consider a cyber vacation."

"Facebook makes our lives so much easier as divorce lawyers," he adds. "Some people give it to us on a silver platter. There are spouses who list themselves as single while they are still married."

Lawyers and recruiters aren't alone in tapping into Facebook's vast database. Despite the uproar last year over Facebook's sharing of user data with some websites, the service recently proposed allowing developers of its more than 550,000 apps to request and obtain users' home addresses and phone numbers. The proposal prompted howls from several members of Congress.

Concerns About Privacy

"This information is extremely sensitive, and the policy Facebook proposed would force users to give up this info if they want an app," says Sen. Al Franken (D-Minn.), who heads the new Senate Subcommittee on Privacy, Technology and the Law. "The potential for fraud is just too great." Franken and three other senators noted in a letter to Facebook that a phone number and a home address, coupled with a small fee paid to a "people search" website, could yield enough information to complete a credit card application in someone else's name.

Franken told us that he's particularly concerned about the potential violation of children's privacy if Facebook implements that policy. "Kids should not be able to give that information away to strangers even if they wanted to."

Facebook recently began testing a program to use status updates and other information to deliver highly targeted ads. So if you post that you're looking for a car, you might find ads from auto dealers peppering the screen. Some might welcome such customization, but others might consider it an invasion of privacy. Regardless, such plans raise questions about what else the service hopes to do with the immense database of personal information it controls. Consumers' concerns might be allayed if they had more of a say in what Facebook does with their personal information.

Facebook publishes privacy policies like other companies do, but as a private corporation it needn't file the annual reports and other disclosures required of publicly held firms such as Microsoft and Google, which can provide even more information about a company.

Whatever the company's obligations, Franken told us, "Facebook needs to make its users' privacy a top priority."

"*[Flash mobs have] taken a darker twist as criminals exploit the anonymity of crowds, using social networking to coordinate everything from robberies to fights to general chaos.*"

Flash Mobs, No Longer Just Dance Parties and Pillow Fights, Pose Growing Criminal Threat: Cops

Eric Tucker and Thomas Watkins

Flash mobs, a large group of people mobilized by social media to meet in a public place, are no longer meeting for fun or to entertain but to commit crimes, claim Associated Press reporters Eric Tucker and Thomas Watkins in the following viewpoint. In fact, the authors maintain, the August 2011 rioting and looting in London was mobilized by youth using Twitter as well as text and instant messaging. Some are mobilizing large groups to target retail stores, Tucker and Watkins assert. That these groups can communicate and gather so quickly makes it very difficult for the police to act, the authors reason.

As you read, consider the following questions:

1. According to Tucker and Watkins, what are some of the peaceful and humorous acts flash mobs used to perform when they started in 2003?

2. What do Twitter officials warn about sharing information about the company's users with law enforcement?

3. What has the Philadelphia Police Department done to help officers prevent flash mob crimes?

The July 4 fireworks display in the Cleveland suburb of Shaker Heights was anything but a family affair.

As many as 1,000 teenagers, mobilized through social networking sites, turned out and soon started fighting and disrupting the event.

Thanks to social networks like Twitter and Facebook, more and more so-called flash mobs are materializing across the globe, leaving police scrambling to keep tabs on the spontaneous assemblies. On Tuesday night, Britain was bracing for a fourth night of rioting as youths used BlackBerry cell phones to mobilize.

One looter's text message before the violence spread read: "If you're down for making money, we're about to go hard in east London."

Flash mobs started off in 2003 as peaceful and often humorous acts of public performance, such as mass dance routines or street pillow fights. But in recent years, the term has taken a darker twist as criminals exploit the anonymity of crowds, using social networking to coordinate everything from robberies to fights to general chaos.

"They're gathering with an intent behind it—not just to enjoy the event," Shaker Heights police chief D. Scott Lee said. "All too often, some of the intent is malicious."

In London, rioting and looting was blamed in part on groups of youths using Twitter, mobile phone text messages and instant messaging on BlackBerry to organize and keep a step ahead of police. BlackBerry's manufacturer, Research In Motion, issued a statement offering empathy for the rioting victims.

"We have engaged with the authorities to assist in any way we can," the statement said.

And Sunday in Philadelphia, Mayor Michael Nutter condemned the behavior of teenagers involved in flash mobs that have left several people injured in recent weeks.

"What is making this unique today is the social media aspect," said Everett Gillison, Philadelphia's deputy mayor for public safety. "They can communicate and congregate at a moment's notice. That can overwhelm any municipality."

A Philadelphia man was assaulted by a group of about 30 people who were believed to have gotten together through Twitter. In 2009, crowds swelled along the trendy South Street shopping district and assaulted several people.

On June 23, a couple dozen youths arrived via subway in Upper Darby, outside Philadelphia, and looted several hundred dollars of sneakers, socks and wrist watches from a Sears store. Their haul wasn't especially impressive but the sheer size of the group and the speed of the roughly five-minute operation made them all but impossible to stop.

"The good thing is there were no weapons and nobody tried to stop them, either," Upper Darby police chief Michael Chitwood said. "The only people that tried to stop them were the police when they rounded them up."

Dubbed "flash mob robberies," the thefts are bedeviling both police and retailers, who say some of the heists were orchestrated or at least boasted about afterward on social networking sites.

In recognition of the problem, the National Retail Federation issued a report last week recommending steps stores can

"So, what's this flashmob all about, and who organised it?," cartoon by Len Hawkins. www.CartoonStock.com.

take to ward off the robberies. There have even been legislative efforts to criminalize flash mobs.

The Cleveland City Council passed a bill to make it illegal to use social media to organize a violent and disorderly flash mob, though the mayor vetoed the measure after the ACLU of Ohio promised it would be unconstitutional. The bill was at least partly inspired by the Shaker Heights disturbances on July 4.

Social networking and technology companies often have policies for coordinating with law enforcement authorities.

Twitter, for example, says it requires a court order or subpoena to share non-public information about its users with law enforcement—including protected tweets. But company officials also warn they can't review the more than 200 million tweets sent daily on the website and that some of the information may be inaccurate if a user has created a fake or anonymous profile.

Jonathan Taplin, director of the innovation lab at the University of Southern California's Annenberg School for Communication, said he was not surprised to see people using social media for organizing flash mob robberies.

"You are essentially having a world where you have 25 million people who are underemployed and 2 percent of the population doing better than they ever have," Taplin said. "Why wouldn't that lead to some sort of social unrest? Why wouldn't people use the latest technologies to effect that?"

In Los Angeles last month, thousands of ravers forced rush-hour street closures when they descended on a Hollywood cinema after a DJ tweeted he was holding a free block party. The sudden crowd dispersed only after police fired bean-bag bullets at the restive revelers and arrested three.

And in April, a man was shot when hundreds of rival gang members congregated along the Los Angeles seafront in Venice, sparking pandemonium as people scattered for cover. The group had gathered after some of them posted on Twitter and police were still strategizing their response to the huge crowd when shots rang out.

Los Angeles Police Capt. Jon Peters said law enforcement's challenge is to try to sift the ocean of tweets and Facebook updates for signs of trouble.

"We need to be able to get better on the intelligence side to pick up on communications that are going on," he said.

Gillison, the deputy mayor from Philadelphia, said the police department there has reached out to younger community members and friended some of them on Facebook. This enables officers to monitor the traffic that could generate flash mobs and some have been prevented, he said.

In April, about 20 teenagers entered G-Star Raw, a high-end men's clothing store in the Dupont Circle neighborhood of the District of Columbia, and stole about $20,000 worth of merchandise despite employees' efforts to grab the apparel back, store manager Greg Lennon said. D.C. police have investigated leads but have not made arrests in the case.

Lennon said he later saw Twitter postings, apparently written after the robbery, that referenced the theft, with one person describing having been in the store and making plans to come back.

The National Retail Federation said 10 percent of 106 companies it surveyed reported being targeted in the last year by groups of thieves using flash mob tactics.

"Retailers are raising red flags about criminal flash mobs, which are wreaking havoc on their business, causing concerns about the safety of their customers and employees, and directly impacting their bottom line," the federation said in a report, which advises retailers to monitor social media networks and report planned heists to the police.

That's exactly what Lennon does. He says he checks his store's Facebook page to see who's visiting and monitors Twitter for any reference to his store and its merchandise.

Gillison and others blame at least part of the problem on bad parenting.

"They're 12 years old and not around the corner from their home. Where's their parents?" said Chitwood, the Upper Darby police chief. "If they're out doing flash mob thefts when they're 12, what the hell are they going to be doing when they're 16?"

| *"Technology makes it even harder to escape domestic abuse."*

Domestic Abusers Use Technology to Stalk and Threaten Their Victims

Dalia Colón

In the following viewpoint, Dalia Colón tells the story of Bella and her abuser, Eddie, to illustrate the many ways in which abusers use technology to stalk and abuse intimate partners. For example, Eddie posted negative comments about Bella while impersonating their daughter on her social networking page, the author asserts. Using "spoofing," Eddie created a website in Bella's name and posted comments that Bella believes led to her being fired, Colón claims. The key, the author maintains, is to keep physical records as evidence of the abuse. Colón is a multimedia reporter focusing on health trends for a collaborative of public broadcasting stations in Florida.

As you read, consider the following questions:

1. In Colón's view, to what do flashing warnings on domestic violence websites alert abuse victims?

2. How do abusers get victims to automatically install remote key logger software, in the author's opinion?

3. According to the author, why is cyber stalking harder to prosecute than actual physical abuse?

It started in New York. Bella was 14. Eddie was 18. They began dating, and almost immediately Eddie became physically abusive.

Bella, 32, who now lives in Pasco County, Fla., can't recall the first incident. She says the abuse was so frequent that she only remembers the "big, big stuff," like the time Eddie body-slammed her into the street in front of her classmates.

Over the years, their relationship was on again, off again. The couple had two daughters and moved to Georgia, and all the while, Eddie abused Bella physically and psychologically. Things escalated when he took the abuse high-tech.

After a few years, he left Bella, moved to Maryland and married one of Bella's former classmates. But that didn't stop Eddie from terrorizing Bella through the Internet.

Cyber-stalking is nothing new. Troll the web for information on domestic violence, and you'll notice something: Many sites contain cautions like WARNING and IMPORTANT PRIVACY NOTICE.

These flashing messages alert victims to a terrifying reality: Technology makes it even harder to escape domestic abuse.

"I've seen it change considerably over the last five years," says Special Agent Anthony Maez, a stalking expert with the New Mexico attorney general's office. "Technology is being used more to track the victim and stalk them, monitor anywhere that they go."

Scary stuff. If you're in an abusive relationship like Bella, then it's important to understand how abusers pervert technology so you can plan a safe escape.

Monitoring Electronic Banking

Account information. How it works: If you share a bank account with your abuser, then he (or she) can easily monitor your spending through the ATM, phone and online. For instance, he can see if you make a deposit on a new apartment. Solution: "People forget that the person they're trying to escape from knows a lot about them," said Maez, the New Mexico special agent. Open a separate account with a password and PIN your abuser won't guess. Use it to build up your escape fund.

Abusing the Internet

Internet history. How it works: A web browser tracks the sites you visit. When your abuser logs on, he can click on the "history" tab to see where you've been online. Solution: Change your browser settings. In Internet Explorer, go to the "tools" menu and click on "InPrivate Browsing." In Firefox, go to the "tools" menu and click on "Start Private Browsing."

Keystroke logger. How it works: This tiny device looks similar to a thumb drive. It records every keystroke entered into a computer. The abuser plugs the logger into the computer's USB port or keyboard. Then when he loads the logger into his own computer, he gets a log of everything you've typed, such as e-mails and passwords. The logger also periodically takes screenshots. Solution: Always check computer ports to ensure there are no external devices attached.

Remote key logger. How it works: This is like a keystroke logger. But rather than installing a tangible device, the abuser sends the logging software as an e-mail attachment. When you download the attachment, you automatically install the logger software. Your Internet activity is sent to the abuser remotely. Solution: Be cautious about what attachments you open, even when using a public computer. "If you feel that your computer is being monitored externally, remotely, then I would definitely involve law enforcement and ask them to do an exam on your computer," says Maez, the stalking expert.

Social networking. How it works: Eddie and Bella's older daughter, Eve [names have been changed] is an aspiring singer and rapper. A few years ago, Eddie created a Facebook page to promote the girl's music. But he began using the site as a way to get under Bella's skin. Eddie would log on and impersonate Eve, posting negative comments about Bella. Solution: Print out screenshots as evidence.

Using Electronic Disguises

Spoofing. How it works: The abuser uses software to disguise himself as, say, your mother. When your phone rings, it looks like your mom's number calling. Harmless enough, right? But when you pick up the phone, it's your abuser on the other end. A related tactic is e-mail spoofing; the abuser disguises his identify in the "sender" field. In Bella's case, Eddie created a Hotmail account and website in her name. The site included comments like I am a child abuser, as well as Bella's name and address. Subsequently, Bella was fired from her job. "What a coincidence," she says. "I was doing auto financing. Now I'm cleaning toilets." Solution: Contact law enforcement. A 2010 law makes caller ID spoofing illegal nationwide.

The Use of Surveillance

Baby monitor. How it works: Your abuser eavesdrops on your conversations from the next room. Solution: When a loved one or social worker visits, suggest going for a walk or to a coffee shop where you can talk freely. If this is not an option, use a note or gesture to communicate that you're in danger.

Wiretapping. How it works: When Bella was living in Georgia, a masked intruder broke into her house and attacked her with an iron. She believes it was Eddie. When she called to confront Eddie about the incident, he recorded the call and used it against her. Solution: In Florida, it's illegal to record a

A Comparison of Off-Line and Online Stalking

Major Similarities

- The majority of cases involve stalking by former intimates, although stranger stalking occurs in the real world and in cyberspace.

- Most victims are women; most stalkers are men.

- Stalkers are generally motivated by the desire to control the victim.

Major Differences

- Off-line stalking generally requires the perpetrator and the victim to be in the same geographic area; cyberstalkers may be across the street or across the country.

- Electronic communication technologies make it much easier for a cyberstalker to encourage third parties to harass or threaten a victim (e.g., a stalker will impersonate the victim and post inflammatory messages on bulletin boards and in chat rooms, causing viewers of these messages to send threatening messages back to the victim).

- Electronic communication technologies also lower the barriers to harassment and threats; a cyberstalker does not need to physically confront the victim.

US Department of Justice, Office of Justice Programs, Office on Violence Against Women, "Offline Versus Online Stalking: A Comparison," Stalking and Domestic Violence: A Report to Congress, May 2001.

phone call without both parties' consent. If you're using a landline, as Bella was, then your abuser has engaged in illegal wiretapping. On a cell phone, Bluetooth technology allows the abuser to collect data and even record your calls from more than 300 feet away. Turn off discovery mode.

Cyber-Stalking and the Law

1. Treat it as a crime. Bella still lives in Pasco County, Fla., with her daughters, now 14 and 9. She's tried unsuccessfully to file cyber-stalking charges against Eddie. She says law enforcement is giving her the runaround.

"They don't know who's supposed to pick the case up," Bella says. "Where's the crime coming from now?" Is the crime in Florida where Bella lives or Georgia where Eddie lives?

"The actual proper venue would be Florida because the abuser is having contact with Florida," says Chris Ragano, a Tampa domestic violence attorney. Regardless of where the abuser lives, the victim can prosecute or seek an injunction in the city or county where she resides. In Florida, cyber-stalking is a first-degree misdemeanor punishable by up to a year in county jail. But if you already have a restraining order against your abuser, or if the abuser adds a threat to the victim's family, then the charge gets upgraded to aggravated cyber-stalking—a third-degree felony punishable by up to 15 years in prison.

2. Know the system. It's hard to prosecute things like Bluetooth surveillance because there's no expectation of privacy in public. Things get even trickier at home. "If it's a situation where it's a family computer in the family home, it's just like a file cabinet. Everyone has access to it, and there's no expectation of privacy," Ragano says. "That's why you need to install passwords and things of that nature to prevent the abuser from going onto there. But then they can install those types of software programs that can intercept that, and that's when it crosses the line" into illegal wiretapping.

3. Keep records. Cyber-stalking is harder to prosecute than physical abuse because it's harder to prove. Print out as much evidence as possible to present in court, including text messages, e-mails and screenshots of social networking sites.

Periodical and Internet Sources Bibliography

The following articles have been selected to supplement the diverse views presented in this chapter.

Stephen A. Cox	"Online Fraud Puts Consumers at Risk," *Baltimore Sun*, December 19, 2011.
Robert Faturechi and Andrew Blankstein	"The Game's Tweet Leaves Police Asking How to Call Foul," *Los Angeles Times*, August 15, 2011.
Federal Bureau of Investigation	"Child Predators: The Online Threat Continues to Grow," May 17, 2011. www.fbi.gov.
Patrik Jonsson	"'Flash Mob' Crimes: How Good Are Police at Tracking Down Culprits?," *Christian Science Monitor*, August 22, 2011.
Robert E. Kessler	"Feds Warn Teens About Online Sex Predators," *Newsday* (Melville, NY), October 9, 2011.
Timothy B. Lee	"Judge: Indictment for Twitter Harassment Is Unconstitutional," Ars Technica, December 2011. http://arstechnica.com.
Laurie Penny	"There's More to the Facebook Generation than the Odd Poke," *New Statesman*, July 4, 2011.
Ben Rodgers	"Police Officers Say Online Predators Can Get Information in Variety of Ways," *Jamestown Sun* (North Dakota), May 18, 2011.
Somini Sengupta	"Case of 8,000 Menacing Posts Tests Limits of Twitter Speech," *New York Times*, August 26, 2011.
Amy Summers	"Is Social Networking More Dangerous to Teens than 'Stranger Danger'?," SocialTimes, January 7, 2011. http://socialtimes.com.

CHAPTER 3

Is Internet Activism a Cybercrime?

Chapter Preface

One of several controversies in the debate over Internet activism is whether hacking to expose security flaws is a punishable crime. At the end of the first decade of the new century, the President Barack Obama administration and Congress developed policies to try to keep pace with the increasing ingenuity of cybercriminals and the growing cybercrime problem. "We have to make sure that we have deterrence for those that are doing wrong," argued Ari Schwartz, Internet policy advisor for the National Institute of Standards and Technology. While some praise these proposals, others are more concerned that these laws will punish "good" hackers, who help organizations identify security flaws and improve network security.

While critics recognize that laws are necessary to combat cybercrime, they maintain that strict, overly broad proposals aimed at deterrence may make computers less secure. These analysts assert that laws that punish both "good" hackers, who often call themselves security researchers, and "bad" hackers, who hack networks to steal information for profit, put networks at risk. Brooklyn Law School professor Derek Bambauer cites Germany as an example of the impact of strict cybersecurity laws. "Germany passed a law banning anything that looks like security research [good hacking], and there have been just enough prosecutions to drive all the security people [hackers] out of Germany." Bambauer recommends a shift away from standards that do not distinguish between good and bad hackers.

Protecting the benign intent of good hackers, however, has not been without its problems. In fact, such laws allow some companies to hide their security flaws. The Digital Millennium Copyright Act (DMCA), a 1998 law designed to protect copyrighted material from digital pirates, contains a measure that protects hackers employed by security companies. However, Bambauer fears that this specific exemption also allows companies that do not hire security companies to go after benign hackers who reveal security flaws that might be embarrassing to the company. Critics point to the lawsuit brought by Sony Computer Entertainment America as a good example. The company filed a suit against George Hotz, who published, online, how he had hacked the Sony PlayStation 3 so that it could run non-Sony software. In the words of attorneys Corynne McSherry and Marcia Hofmann of the Electronic Frontier Foundation, the lawsuit sends "a message to security researchers around the world; publish the details of our security flaws and we'll come after you with both barrels blazing." Thus, these critics conclude, companies will punish users who access their computers in ways they do not like, even if the intent is not criminal.

Whether cybercrime laws unfairly target good-guy hackers and threaten the security of consumers remains controversial. The authors in the following chapter present their views on whether or not Internet activism is a cybercrime. How technology industries and the government will respond to ever-present hackers is unclear. However, when technology giant Microsoft released its motion-sensing Kinect game controller, hackers almost immediately devised new uses for the hardware. Jason Tanz of *Wired* reported that Microsoft's response to these hacks went from "hostility to acceptance to vigorous support" within months. Perhaps this is a sign of attitudes to come.

"Now governments have to worry about conducting diplomacy while looking over their shoulders for hacktivists who have raised transparency to the level of dogma."

Activist Websites That Reveal Sensitive Documents Threaten Diplomatic Negotiations

John Feffer

Secret diplomatic discussions are necessary so that antagonistic governments such as China, North Korea, and the United States can forge politically beneficial agreements, argues John Feffer in the following viewpoint. When activist organizations such as WikiLeaks air negative comments made by diplomatic participants, they threaten this process, he maintains. While the statements aired may be true, diplomacy requires that people sometimes outwardly say things they do not inwardly believe to come to mutually beneficial agreements, Feffer claims. Unfortunately, WikiLeaks places transparency above the realities of diplomacy, he concludes. Feffer is codirector of Foreign Policy in Focus at the Institute for Policy Studies, a progressive think tank.

John Feffer, "Transparency Fundamentalists," *Foreign Policy in Focus: World Beat*, vol. 5, no. 47, November 30, 2010. http://www.fpif.org. Copyright © 2010 by the Institute for Policy Studies. All rights reserved. Reproduced by permission.

As you read, consider the following questions:

1. What led Feffer to the conclusion that the transparency fundamentalists may have gone too far?

2. In the author's opinion, why should secret discussions among China, North Korea, and the United States be immediate?

3. In the author's opinion, what might complicate any diplomatic efforts to defuse the current standoff in northeast Asia more than China's doubts about North Korea?

WikiLeaks[1] puts the government through a full body scanner to reveal many dirty secrets. U.S. officials, not surprisingly, have responded with anger. They don't want their "junk" [private parts] exposed or touched. No one, from emperors to excursionists, likes to be naked in public. And the latest revelations are the most intrusive yet. It's one thing when WikiLeaks exposes the lies of the U.S. government in Afghanistan or Iraq. But with this Sunday's [November 28, 2010] release of 251,287 U.S. embassy cables, what the website calls "the largest set of confidential documents ever to be released into the public domain," perhaps the transparency fundamentalists have gone too far.

Why Secret Negotiations Are Necessary

To explain why, let's first go to northeast Asia where the North Korean government has indulged in its own form of transparency by revealing its uranium enrichment facility to visiting U.S. guests. At the same time, North Korea very clearly announced its objection to South Korean military exercises conducted in the area around the Northern Limit Line (NLL), the

---

1. WikiLeaks publishes documents otherwise unavailable to the public from anonymous sources whose identity is protected. A wiki allows any user to add or edit content, but the site now follows a more traditional publishing model, accepting submissions that are vetted by staff members and volunteers from mainstream news media.

disputed maritime boundary between the two countries. When South Korea went ahead with those drills, including live artillery fire, North Korea shelled Yeonpyeong Island near the NLL, killing two civilians and two soldiers. To be sure, this was a disproportionate response. But North Korea's response wasn't entirely unexpected.

Nevertheless, speculation abounds concerning the motives behind North Korea's attack. According to the pundits, Pyongyang [the capital of North Korea] wanted to get back at Seoul [the capital of South Korea] for holding the G20 [group of finance ministers and central bank governors from twenty major economies] summit and stealing all the headlines. Or, it wanted to strengthen the hand of Kim Jong-un, the youngest son of leader Kim Jong-il and the designated successor. [2] Or, it wanted to jolt the United States out of its policy of "strategic patience." Any of the above might be true. Someday, should it have a go at the North Korean archives, WikiLeaks might provide a full answer. In the interim, it seems that North Korea simply followed through on its stated intention to retaliate against South Korea's military exercises.

South Korea and the United States have gone ahead with military exercises in the same area. The United States sent over an aircraft carrier loaded with 75 aircraft and 6,000 sailors that, along with South Korean forces, have been conducting military exercises near this disputed maritime border. This isn't just waving the big stick of deterrence. It's inserting the stick directly into the hornet's nest. When the hornets buzz and sting, the stick wielder bears a portion of the responsibility.

Even proponents of a harder-line stance admit that this isn't much of a strategy. "The only conceivable (but also useless) reply is tough talk and a show of military power," writes North Korea expert Andrei Lankov. "This is also some-

2. Kim Jong-il died on December 17, 2011, and his son Kim Jong-un succeeded him as leader of North Korea.

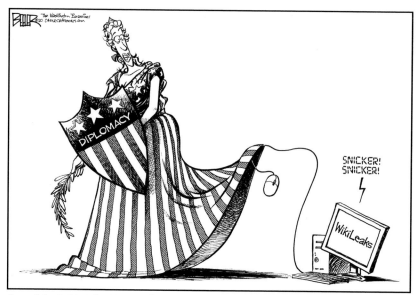

Copyright © 2010, by Nate Beeler, The Columbus Dispatch, and CagleCartoons.com.

what dangerous since it will increase the likelihood of inci-
dental clashes on the border. But one has to understand: The
government has to show that it is doing something when actually nothing can be done."

A Tight Position

The South Korean government is indeed in a tight position.
The Lee Myung-bak administration was elected on a conservative platform of talking and acting tougher toward North
Korea. It has largely followed through on this agenda. But
hard-liners in the south want the Lee administration to strike
back against North Korea. It's truly a tough line to toe—
acting tough and not triggering a second Korean War. Lee
"should shut out the voices that would decry 'rewarding bad
behavior' or 'appeasing North Korea' by seeking further engagement now," writes Foreign Policy in Focus contributor Peter Certo in the *Focal Points Blog*. Fortunately, South Korea
backed away at the last minute from its pledge to repeat its

live ammunition exercise in the very same location that triggered North Korea's disproportionate response.

The United States is supporting South Korea and pressuring China to restrain its erstwhile ally. Neither of these strategies is particularly effective. By sending an aircraft carrier into the disputed waters, the United States angers not only North Korea but China as well. And even if China were disposed to rein in its ally—and there are lots of reasons why China won't do anything to seriously destabilize the current government in Pyongyang—it doesn't have as much influence as Washington believes (and wants) it to have. North Korea is the Israel of northeast Asia. It acts according to its own national security imperatives and listens to its big brother ally only when the advice confirms its own assumptions.

A Need for Secret Discussions

Instead, the United States should sit down with China and North Korea for some immediate, secret discussions to ratchet down the tensions. They should be immediate because the risk of war is very high. And they should be secret because the negotiators need the time and space to discuss sensitive details and work out some kind of understanding, far from the prying eyes of journalists, the political opposition, and an easily outraged public.

Which brings us back to WikiLeaks. It's one thing when leaked documents complicate the execution of war. It's quite another when they complicate the execution of diplomacy. The current trove of material reveals negative comments by Saudi Arabia about Pakistani leader Asif Ali Zardari and by Israel about Turkish leader Recep Tayyip Erdogan. . . . These sentiments might be true, but diplomacy is all about saying one thing and believing another—all for the purposes of getting to yes. Like Vegas, what happens in diplomacy sometimes should just stay in diplomacy.

A Data Dump Without Context

You might object that WikiLeaks is just turbo-charged journalism. But journalists are careful to assess leaks for their likely veracity and then place the revealed information in a larger context. WikiLeaks bypasses the intermediaries and performs a big data dump, the raw and the cooked all mixed together. Some of the material simply confirms publicly what governments believe privately. For instance, the information in WikiLeaks about North Korean missile sales to Iran suggests that the long-standing commercial relationship between the two countries—North Korea has been selling Iran missiles since the late 1980s—has been upgraded technologically.

But this is data, not diplomacy. More troubling are the revelations about China's doubts concerning its North Korean neighbor. It's not the doubts themselves so much as the airing of them in U.S. cables that might complicate any diplomatic efforts to defuse the current standoff. Worse would be, in some future WikiLeaks cache, the exposing of secret negotiations with North Korea to prepare a comprehensive deal. It's hard enough to keep journalists at arm's length in order to conclude negotiations like the Oslo accords [attempts to resolve the ongoing Israeli-Palestinian conflict] or the denuclearization negotiations with Libya, both of which required utmost secrecy and delicacy. Now governments have to worry about conducting diplomacy while looking over their shoulders for hacktivists who have raised transparency to the level of dogma.

Civic activists pursue "sunshine laws" to expose backroom deals and corrupting collusion. WikiLeaks takes the sunshine law into its own hands in order to expose the shadowy corners of foreign policy. The result is always fascinating, often illuminating, and sometimes politically useful. But there are limits. As those who suffer from skin cancer can tell you, too much sunlight can also be deadly.

> "WikiLeaks has been involved in a fruitful collaboration, a new form of hybrid journalism emerging in the space between so-called hacktivists and mainstream media."

Activist Websites That Reveal Sensitive Documents Are a Useful Form of Journalism

David Carr

In the following viewpoint, David Carr claims that WikiLeaks, an organization that publishes secret documents, represents a new, hybrid form of journalism. By being more selective in the documents it releases and allowing mainstream media to review and report on these documents before publishing them, WikiLeaks adds value to the content, he reasons. Nevertheless, Carr maintains, some claim WikiLeaks' goal is to embarrass people in power and expose corrupt governments, not report news. Indeed, he argues, WikiLeaks sees transparency as the ultimate goal, while mainstream media outlets generally recognize that governments have the right to keep some secrets. Carr writes on media issues for the New York Times.

As you read, consider the following questions:

1. How did WikiLeaks founder Julian Assange create a comfort zone for his partners in journalism, according to Carr?

2. In what way is WikiLeaks being denied the same protections given other media outlets in free countries, in the author's view?

3. According to Steve Coll, what must WikiLeaks do to prevent the clock from running out on collaboration with media outlets?

Has WikiLeaks[1] changed journalism forever?

Perhaps. Or maybe it was the other way around.

Think back to 2008, when WikiLeaks simply released documents that suggested the government of Kenya had looted its country. The follow-up in the mainstream media was decidedly muted.

Then last spring [in 2010], WikiLeaks adopted a more journalistic approach—editing and annotating a 2007 video from Baghdad in which an Apache helicopter fired on men who appeared to be unarmed, including two employees of Reuters. The reviews were mixed, with some suggesting that the video had been edited to political ends, but the disclosure received much more attention in the press.

Partnering with Media

In July, WikiLeaks began what amounted to a partnership with mainstream media organizations, including the *New York Times*, by giving them an early look at the so-called Afghan

1. WikiLeaks publishes documents otherwise unavailable to the public from anonymous sources whose identity is protected. A wiki allows any user to add or edit content, but the site now follows a more traditional publishing model, accepting submissions that are vetted by staff members and volunteers from mainstream news media.

War Diary, a strategy that resulted in extensive reporting on the implications of the secret documents.

Then in November, the heretofore classified mother lode of 250,000 United States diplomatic cables that describe tensions across the globe was shared by WikiLeaks with *Le Monde, El País*, the *Guardian* and *Der Spiegel*.[2] (The *Guardian* shared documents with the *New York Times*.) The result was huge: Many articles have come out since, many of them deep dives into the implications of the trove of documents.

Notice that with each successive release, WikiLeaks has become more strategic and has been rewarded with deeper, more extensive coverage of its revelations. It's a long walk from WikiLeaks's origins as a user-edited site held in common to something more akin to a traditional model of publishing, but seems to be in keeping with its manifesto to deliver documents with "maximum possible impact."

Julian Assange, WikiLeaks's founder and guiding spirit, apparently began to understand that scarcity, not ubiquity, drives coverage of events. Instead of just pulling back the blankets for all to see, he began to limit the disclosures to those who would add value through presentation, editing and additional reporting. In a sense, Mr. Assange, a former programmer, leveraged the processing power of the news media to build a story and present it in comprehensible ways. (Of course, as someone who draws a paycheck from a mainstream journalism outfit, it may be no surprise that I continue to see durable value in what we do even amid the journalistic jujitsu WikiLeaks introduces.)

Anarchism or Journalism?

And by publishing only a portion of the documents, rather than spilling information willy-nilly and recklessly endanger-

---

2. All widely read foreign newspapers, *Le Monde* is published in France, *El País* in Spain, the *Guardian* in Great Britain, and *Der Spiegel* in Germany.

ing lives, WikiLeaks could also strike a posture of responsibility, an approach that seems to run counter to Mr. Assange's own core anarchism.

Although Mr. Assange is now arguing that the site is engaged in what he called a new kind of "scientific journalism," his earlier writings suggest he believes the mission of WikiLeaks is to throw sand in the works of what he considers corrupt, secretive and inherently evil states. He initiated a conspiracy in order to take down what he saw as an even greater conspiracy.

"WikiLeaks is not a news organization, it is a cell of activists that is releasing information designed to embarrass people in power," said George Packer, a writer on international affairs at the *New Yorker*. "They simply believe that the State Department is an illegitimate organization that needs to be exposed, which is not really journalism."

By shading his radicalism and collaborating with mainstream outlets, Mr. Assange created a comfort zone for his partners in journalism. They could do their jobs, and he could do his.

"The notion that this experience has somehow profoundly changed journalism, the way that information gets out or changed the way that diplomacy happens, seems rather exaggerated," said Bill Keller, the executive editor of the *New York Times*, which used information from the leaks to report a series of large articles.

"It was a big deal, but not an unfamiliar one. Consumers of information became privy to a lot of stuff that had been secret before," Mr. Keller said. "The scale of it was unusual, but was it different in kind from the Pentagon Papers [US Department of Defense history of the US political-military involvement in Vietnam from 1945 to 1967] or revelation of Abu Ghraib [US military abuse of prisoners at Abu Ghraib prison in Iraq] or government eavesdropping? I think probably not."

In this case, the media companies could also take some comfort in knowing that the current trove did not contain, with a few notable exceptions, any earthshaking revelations. No thinking citizen was surprised to learn that diplomats don't trust each other and say so behind closed doors. But as it has became increasingly apparent that WikiLeaks was changing the way information is released and consumed, questions were raised about the value of traditional journalistic approaches.

"People from the digital world are always saying we don't need journalists at all because information is everywhere and there in no barrier to entry," said Nicholas Lemann, dean of the Columbia Journalism School. "But these documents provide a good answer to that question. Even though journalists didn't dig them out, there is a great deal of value in their efforts to explain and examine them. Who else would have had the energy or resources to do what these news organization have done?"

Lacking Traditional Media Protections

WikiLeaks certainly isn't being afforded the same protections we give other media outlets in free countries. It has come under significant attack as PayPal, Amazon and Visa have all tried to bar WikiLeaks from their services, a move that would seem unthinkable had it been made against mainstream newspapers. (Can you imagine the outcry if a credit card company decided to cut off the *Washington Post* because it didn't like what was on the front page?)

Sen. Joseph Lieberman has said that Mr. Assange should be charged with treason while [former governor and vice presidential nominee] Sarah Palin has called him "an anti-American operative with blood on his hands." (Indeed, Senator Lieberman has suggested that the Justice Department should examine the role of the *New York Times* in the leaks.)

Mr. Packer is very much against the prosecution of WikiLeaks on grounds of treason because, he said, "discerning the legal difference between what WikiLeaks did and what news organizations do is difficult and would set a terrible precedent."

A Complicated Partner

But Mr. Assange, who is in jail in Britain in connection with a Swedish extradition request, is a complicated partner. So far, WikiLeaks has been involved in a fruitful collaboration, a new form of hybrid journalism emerging in the space between so-called hacktivists and mainstream media outlets, but the relationship is an unstable one.

WikiLeaks may be willing to play ball with newspapers for now, but the organization does not share the same values or objectives. Mr. Assange and the site's supporters see transparency as the ultimate objective, believing that sunshine and openness will deprive bad actors of the secrecy they require to be successful. Mainstream media may spend a lot of time trying to ferret information out of official hands, but they largely operate in the belief that the state is legitimate and entitled to at least some of its secrets.

And Mr. Assange has placed a doomsday card on the table: He has said that if WikiLeaks's existence is threatened, the organization would be willing to spill all the documents in its possession out into the public domain, ignoring the potentially mortal consequences. (His lawyers told ABC News that they expect he will be indicted on espionage charges in the United States.) Mr. Packer said such an act "is something no journalistic organization would ever do, or threaten to do."

And what if WikiLeaks was unhappy with how one of its ad hoc media partners had handled the information it provided or became displeased with the coverage of WikiLeaks? The same guns in the info-war that have been aimed at its political and Web opponents could be trained on media outlets.

An Open Question

Steve Coll, president of the New America Foundation and an author and a contributor to the *New Yorker* who has written extensively about Afghanistan, said that the durability of the WikiLeaks model remained an open question.

"I'm skeptical about whether a release of this size is ever going to take place again," he said, "in part because established interests and the rule of law tend to come down pretty hard on incipient movements. Think of the initial impact of Napster and what subsequently happened to them."

Of course, Napster is no longer around but the insurgency it represented all but tipped the music industry.

"Right now, media outlets are treating this as a transaction with a legitimate journalistic organization," he said. "But at some point, they are going to have to evolve into an organization that has an address and identity or the clock will run out on that level of collaboration."

Emily Bell, the director of the Tow Center for Digital Journalism at Columbia Journalism School, said that WikiLeaks had already changed the rules by creating a situation where competitive news organizations were now cooperating to share a scoop.

"WikiLeaks represents a new kind of advocacy, one that brings to mind the activism of the '60s, one in which people want to get their own hands on information and do their own digging," she said. "What you are seeing is just a crack in the door right now. No one can tell where this is really going."

> "Hacktivism is the application of information technologies (and the hacking of them) to political action [and] has ranged from simple website defacings and attempts to unbottle secret information to efforts to ensure the privacy of ordinary citizens."

Some Activists Hack the Internet to Promote Political Beliefs

Peter Ludlow

A movement of activist hackers who mistrust authority and believe in open access to information is growing, claims Peter Ludlow in the following viewpoint. Many use their hacking skills to take political action, he asserts. For example, Ludlow maintains, in the early 1990s the Hong Kong Blondes disrupted Chinese computer networks to give people access to blocked websites, and more recently, the group Anonymous led attacks on Church of Scientology websites to oppose the church's censorship policies. Hacktivists are a large network; thus efforts to topple one person or website will be futile, he concludes. Ludlow, a philosophy professor at Northwestern University, is editor of Crypto Anarchy, Cyberstates, and Pirate Utopias.

As you read, consider the following questions:

1. According to Ludlow, who do many believe is the protagonist of the WikiLeaks controversy?

2. Why does Ludlow claim it will be difficult to disable the WikiLeaks system?

3. In the author's opinion, how should Julian Assange's philosophy and the hacktivist tradition be characterized?

In recent months [fall 2010] there has been considerable discussion about the WikiLeaks[1] phenomenon, and understandably so, given the volume and sensitivity of the documents the website has released. What this discussion has revealed, however, is that the media and government agencies believe there is a single protagonist to be concerned with—something of a James Bond villain, if you will—when in fact the protagonist is something altogether different: an informal network of revolutionary individuals bound by a shared ethic and culture.

According to conventional wisdom, the alleged protagonist is, of course, WikiLeaks founder Julian Assange, and the discussion of him has ranged from Raffi Khatchadourian's June portrait in the *New Yorker*, which makes Assange sound like a master spy in a John le Carré novel, to Tunku Varadarajan's epic ad hominem bloviation on The Daily Beast: "With his bloodless, sallow face, his lank hair drained of all color, his languorous, very un-Australian limbs, and his aura of blinding pallor that appears to admit no nuance, Assange looks every inch the amoral, über-nerd villain."

Misunderstanding WikiLeaks

Some have called for putting Assange "out of business" (even if we must violate international law to do it), while others,

1. WikiLeaks publishes documents otherwise unavailable to the public from anonymous sources whose identity is protected. A wiki allows any user to add or edit content, but the site now follows a more traditional publishing model, accepting submissions that are vetted by staff members and volunteers from mainstream news media.

ranging from Daniel Ellsberg [former US military analyst who released the Pentagon Papers and urges patriotic whistleblowing] to Assange himself, think he is (in Ellsberg's words) "in some danger." I don't doubt that Assange is in danger, but even if he is put out of business by arrest, assassination or character impeachment with charges of sexual misconduct, it would not stanch the flow of secret documents into the public domain. To think otherwise is an error that reflects a colossal misunderstanding of the nature of WikiLeaks and the subculture from which it emerged.

WikiLeaks is not the one-off creation of a solitary genius; it is the product of decades of collaborative work by people engaged in applying computer hacking to political causes, in particular, to the principle that information hoarding is evil— and, as [futurist] Stewart Brand said in 1984, "Information wants to be free." Today there is a broad spectrum of people engaged in this cause, so that were Assange to be eliminated today, WikiLeaks would doubtless continue, and even if WikiLeaks were somehow to be eliminated, new sites would emerge to replace it.

Let's begin by considering whether it is possible to take WikiLeaks off-line, as called for in the *Washington Post* by former [president George W.] Bush speechwriter Marc Thiessen, who added that "taking [Assange] off the streets is not enough; we must also recover the documents he unlawfully possesses and disable the system he has built to illegally disseminate classified information."

Consider the demand that we "recover the documents." Even the documents that have not been made public by WikiLeaks are widely distributed all over the Internet. WikiLeaks has released an encrypted 1.4 gigabyte file called "insurance.aes256." If something happens to Assange, the password to the encrypted file will be released (presumably via a single Twitter tweet). What's in the file? We don't know, but at 1.4 gigabytes, it is nineteen times the size of the Afghan war log that was recently distributed to major newspapers. Legendary hacker Kevin Poulsen speculates that the file "is doubtless in the hands of thousands, if not tens of thousands, of netizens already."

It's also a bit difficult to "disable the system," since WikiLeaks did not need to create a new network; the group simply relied on existing electronic communications networks (e.g., the Internet) and the fact that there are tens of thousands of like-minded people all over the world. Where did all those like-minded people come from? Are they all under the spell of Assange? To the contrary, they were active long before Assange sat down to hack his first computer.

The Hacker Ethic

It has long been an ethical principle of hackers that ideas and information are not to be hoarded but are to be shared. In 1984, when Assange turned 13, Steven Levy described this attitude in his book *Hackers:[Heroes of the Computer Revolution]*. After interviewing a number of hackers, he distilled a "hacker ethic," which included, among others, the following of two maxims: (1) all information should be free; (2) mistrust authority and promote decentralization.

These sentiments were poetically expressed by a hacker named The Mentor, in an essay titled "The Conscience of a Hacker." It was written shortly after his arrest, and appeared in the important hacker publication *Phrack* in 1986.

> We explore . . . and you call us criminals. We seek after knowledge . . . and you call us criminals. We exist without skin color, without nationality, without religious bias . . . and you call us criminals. You build atomic bombs, you wage wars, you murder, cheat, and lie to us and try to make us believe it's for our own good, yet we're the criminals. Yes, I am a criminal. My crime is that of curiosity. My crime is that of judging people by what they say and think, not what they look like. My crime is that of outsmarting you, some-

thing that you will never forgive me for. I am a hacker, and this is my manifesto. You may stop this individual, but you can't stop us all.

Indeed, you can't stop them all. One year after The Mentor's manifesto was published, Assange acquired a modem and entered cyberspace for the first time. In the quarter century since, that basic hacker philosophy has not been abandoned, and indeed has evolved into a broad cultural movement. Hacker conferences with thousands of attendees have sprung up in places ranging from Amsterdam and New York to Las Vegas and Abu Dhabi, and small weekly hacker meet ups are routine in every major city in the world.

The Turn to Hacktivism

For many hackers, this activity has taken a decidedly political turn—into what is sometimes called hacktivism. Hacktivism is the application of information technologies (and the hacking of them) to political action. This has ranged from simple website defacings and attempts to unbottle secret information to efforts to ensure the privacy of ordinary citizens by providing them military-grade encryption (a successful mission of the infamous Cypherpunks).

Hacktivism has been extended to political action against all manner of power structures. One of the earliest examples is the Hong Kong Blondes—a group that disrupted computer networks in China in the 1990s so people could get access to blocked websites. The Hong Kong Blondes were in turn assisted by a Texas-based hacker group called the Cult of the Dead Cow (cDc), which helped them with advanced encryption technology. In 2006 the cDc subsequently waged a PR [public relations] campaign against Google (calling it Goolag) when Google caved in to Chinese censorship demands. Their slogan: "Goolag: Exporting censorship, one search at a time."

Examples of hacktivism by other groups have included denizens of the rowdy, transgressive and scatological 4chan

The Span of Hacktivism

2002   A virtual sit-in crashes the World Economic Forum.

2003   Voice of America announces its new anti-censorship software project.

2004   Pro-Linux hacktivists target the software company SCO with MyDoom virus.

2006   Electronic Disturbance Theater and Hacklab hold virtual sit-ins to protest the massacre in Atenco, Mexico.

2007   Electronic Disturbance Theater stages a virtual sit-in against Michigan legislature in response to cuts in Medicaid.

2008   Anonymous knocks Church of Scientology website off-line in opposition to its policy of secrecy.

2009   Anonymous sets up Anonymous Iran to support Iranian election protests.

2010   Anonymous disrupts service on Australian government websites in response to attempts to filter the Internet.

2011   Anonymous attacks government websites in Tunisia, Egypt, and Syria in support of dissidents.

2012   Anonymous slows Department of Justice and FBI websites in response to shutdown of file sharing website Megaupload.

Some hacktivism noted above may be attributed to a hacktivist group that claimed responsibility but was not in fact responsible for the attack.

Compiled by editor.

website, operating under the name Anonymous, in its assault on attempted censorship by the Church of Scientology, using a series of denial-of-service attacks against Scientology websites. Anonymous also moved against the Iranian government during the 2009 elections, when it established a website that shared information from inside Iran and provided advice to Iranian activists on how to encrypt and safely transmit communications. Another notable example is a group of Portuguese hackers called Urban KaOs, which protested the Indonesian government's treatment of East Timor by hacking Indonesian government websites in the 1990s and posting alternative pages that protested the government's policies.

A Call for Openness

The political compass of these hacktivist groups has never pointed true right or true left—at least by our typical way of charting the political landscape. They have been consistently unified in their adherence to the basic hacker principles as outlined by Levy and The Mentor in the 1980s: Information should not be hoarded by powerful constituencies—it needs to be placed in the hands of the general public. This principle is followed even to the point of threatening to become a "foolish consistency"—as in the recent document dump from WikiLeaks, which drew the rebuke of five human rights organizations, including Amnesty International, because, they felt, civilian sources were not adequately protected.

As described in Khatchadourian's *New Yorker* profile, Assange's philosophy blends in seamlessly with the hacktivist tradition: It can't be characterized in terms of left versus right so much as individual versus institution. In particular, Assange holds that truth, creativity, etc., are corrupted by institutional hierarchies, or what he calls "patronage networks," and that much of illegitimate power is perpetuated by the hoarding of information.

Meanwhile, in a profile of Army Pvt. Bradley Manning, the man accused of leaking documents to WikiLeaks, the *New York Times* considered many explanations for what Manning did. He was troubled because "classmates made fun of him for being gay"; he was "ignored" by his superiors; he was "self-medicating." Curiously elided was what Manning actually said his motivation was. In a May 25 conversation, the hacker Adrian Lamo asked Manning why he gave the information to WikiLeaks when he could have sold it to Russia or China and "made bank [earned a lot of money]." Manning replied in true hacktivist fashion, "Because it's public data . . . it belongs in the public domain . . . information should be free . . . if it's out in the open . . . it should [do the] public good."

The traditional media, governments and their security organizations just cannot get unglued from the idea that there must be a single mastermind behind an operation like WikiLeaks. While this model works great in fictional dramas, it does not track what is really happening. This is not a one-man or even one-group operation. It is a network of thousands motivated by a shared hacktivist culture and ethic. And with or without Assange, it is not going away.

> "[The hacktivist group Anonymous] is looking less like a force and more like an incoherent rabble . . . when many of its ideals have been washed away in a tide of misdirected hacking."

Some Activist Hackers Have Become Too Corrupt to Be Effective

Charles Arthur

Internet activist organizations such as Anonymous and Lulz Security, or LulzSec, are losing favor as an effective political force, even among members, argues Charles Arthur in the following viewpoint. Some oppose the release of innocent victims' personal information during Internet attacks when these organizations claim to value anonymity, he asserts. Others cite the hypocrisy of supporting free speech when hacktivists attack anyone who speaks against them, Arthur claims. The problem these groups face is a lack of organization or rules of political engagement, making them more like a mob than a political force, he reasons. Arthur is a technology editor for the Guardian, *a British newspaper.*

As you read, consider the following questions:

1. How did British Parliament member Louise Mensch respond to Internet threats that purportedly came from Anonymous, as reported by Arthur?

2. How does the author define "doxers"?

3. In the author's opinion, why was leaking personal details of HBGary staff avoidable?

L ouise Mensch, the Conservative MP [member of Parliament], didn't react as perhaps the sender of the threatening e-mail she received on Monday [August 22, 2011] had hoped. She came out swinging—as anyone who knows her even a little might have been able to predict.

"Had some morons from [the hacktivist collectives] Anonymous/LulzSec[1] threaten my children via e-mail. As I'm in the States, be good . . . to have somebody from the UK police advise me where I should forward the e-mail," she tweeted. And then followed up by refusing to be cowed: "I'm posting it on Twitter because they threatened me telling me to get off Twitter. Hi kids!::waves::".

Hacktivist Defections

Sticking two fingers up [an insulting gesture] at Anonymous might have drawn some gasps a while back. (Of course, it's impossible to prove that it really came "from" Anonymous, and many Twitter accounts from members denied the idea: "1. Not discussed in IRC [Internet Relay Chat, the favoured gathering place for Anonymous members]. 2. E-mail & threats of violence not Anon's MO [modus operandi]. 3. @louisemensch is not important enough," tweeted one such, JohnDoeKM.)

1. Anonymous is a term used to describe an anarchic community of online users acting simultaneously; it was later attributed to a hacktivist group responsible for distributed denial-of-service attacks on the websites of institutions it opposes. LulzSec, short for Lulz Security, is a computer hacker group that claimed responsibility for several high-profile computer attacks.

But the group is looking less like a force and more like an incoherent rabble as a result of the past two months, when many of its ideals have been washed away in a tide of misdirected hacking, which in turn has led to a number of public defections by people disaffected with its lack of focus.

As one departing member posted on Pastebin[2] (the favoured site for declarations relating to the group):

> "Anonymous fights for freedom, you don't like people controlling you, that is admirable. But while you fight to remain free from government tyranny, you've shoved your views, into the faces of others. Because of your recent acts you've gone from liberators to terrorist dictators. I'm posting this as a guest because I feel that by simply disagreeing with you, I run a risk of attack."

And here's another (I've tweaked his Capitals For Every Word style):

> So when I started with Anon I thought I was helping people but over the past few months things inside anon have changed. I am mostly talking about Antisec [an anti-security operation being run by Anonymous] and Lulzsec. They both go against what I stand for (and what Anonymous says they stand for). Antisec has released gig after gig of innocent people's information. For what? What did they do? Does Anon have the right to remove the anonymity of innocent people? They are always talking about people's right to remain anonymous, so why are they removing that right?

Or another, from "cornfog":

> They jump on any possible chance they get to make headlines. Do you honestly think anonymous cares about BART[3] ... well of course they don't, why else would they release

2. Pastebin is a web application that allows its users to upload snippets of text, usually samples of source code, for public viewing.
3. BART is short for Bay Area Rapid Transit, which services the San Francisco Bay Area in California.

tons of personal information on innocent users who they are fighting for? Yeah ... what? I don't understand this, but I don't seem to be the only one. Which leads us to our next topic, which would be Freedom Of Speech, another cause anonymous fights for ... until it's a negative comment on them, then they bash you beyond hell and harass you, and your family, for simply speaking out freely, again, something they fight for.

A New Level of Hacking?

You get the idea: Anonymous isn't really winning hearts and minds. But the reason why not—and particularly why not in the past couple of months—is down to a group which you might have thought had taken Anonymous's ideas to a new level. That would be the hacking group LulzSec.

This was the crew gathered from within Anonymous which hacked Sony Pictures Europe, and PBS, and a number of games companies, and then raised their sights to hit the US Senate, and then the UK Serious Organised Crime Agency and finally—after saying they had disbanded—News International's site, planting a fake story claiming [media mogul] Rupert Murdoch was dead, and then redirecting readers of the *Sun* front page to their Twitter feed.

The fun may have stopped, though. In Britain three people have been arrested and two charged with offences relating to LulzSec's actions.

For some time after the UK arrests, the only visibly active member of LulzSec remained its leader, known online as "Sabu", who would simultaneously deny that he was its leader and then use phrases such as "my team". Details about him suggested that he is Puerto Rican, living in New York and—critically—at least 30 years old. That would make him very different from the others said to be involved in LulzSec; the chat logs show that he was the mature one who directed operations. Most of Anonymous's hangers-on tend to range from early teens to early 20s. For almost a month after LulzSec's final hack he remained on Twitter at the @Anonymousabu account, generally either arguing with people or boosting those he backed. (For a period he seemed to share the account with at least one other person: the timings of the postings, with a "double peak" roughly correlating to one person based in Europe, and another on the East Coast of the US, and the multilingual content at particular times, didn't quite tell the story of a single person. But the second "identity" went away in the past couple of weeks.)

Who's Snitching on Whom?

Then came a vicious chat room dispute with Mike "Virus" Nieves, whom Sabu accused of having passed on information to the New York police following a comment he, Sabu, had made about nyc.gov. Sabu denounced Virus on Twitter as a "snitch" and began putting out details about him. Meanwhile, the "doxers"—people in the online world who like to make individuals' details public—began putting together their profiles of Sabu. The most recent ones pulled together a number of details, including photos, e-mails, websites and history for someone who is claimed to be Sabu. Unlike previous "unmaskings", Sabu didn't deny these ones; he simply disappeared, leaving a gnomic tweet echoing *The Usual Suspects* ("The greatest trick the devil ever pulled was convincing the world he did not exist. And like that . . . he is gone.").

He hasn't been visible online since. It's not presently known whether he has been—as they say in hacker circles— "V&". (V + "and" = vanned, or "given a ride in the party wagon": in other words, arrested.)

But Sabu's actions, while he was visible, left a vacuum in Anonymous. One prominent hacker, The Jester—reckoned to be an ex-US military member whose aims are antithetical to those of Anonymous, and who operates on his own targeting what he sees as anti-American jihadist sites (but also, when it released the US diplomatic cables, WikiLeaks)—asserted that

A Glossary of Hacking Terms

Botnet—a network of "zombie" computers taken over without their owners' knowledge to send spam e-mails or attack a website.

Circumvention device—hacker-developed software that allows people to convert electronic media such as DVDs and video games for use on devices other than those originally intended.

DDoS (distributed denial-of-service)—an atack that slows or stops websites or computer servers by bombarding them with data or software from multiple computers.

Hacktivist—someone who uses computers or computer networks as a means of political protest.

Open source—software or electronic devices with original source code that is openly published so others may improve or expand its capabilities and then perhaps freely distribute the modified code.

Social engineering—manipulating people into providing confidential information to break into a computer network.

Scareware—scam software that cybercriminals place on computers to scare users into buying fake anti-virus programs or other products.

Virus—a program that alters a computer's operation without the owner's knowledge and propagates as users forward the file it rides on.

Worm—software that can copy itself and infect multiple computers on a network.

Marcia Clemmitt, "Computer Hacking,"
CQ Researcher, September 16, 2011.

Sabu was doing everything you'd expect of an Islamic cyber-terrorist. Most notably, targeting Western government sites rather than those of Burma, Libya or China or any of a number of arguably more repressive regimes than the US or UK. Sabu denied this vehemently.

The trouble was, LulzSec's aim—to hack for laughs—didn't seem to hold up. The game had gotten serious. Which meanwhile left Anonymous wondering what the hell it was for.

Of course, the thing about Anonymous is that it isn't *exactly* organised, and it doesn't *exactly* have a manifesto; more a *modus operandi*, which is to use computing and networking technologies to protest at what it sees as infringements of what it sees as rights. Sometimes these are spot-on: When the members of the collective used their power to overturn attempts by the Church of Scientology to suppress discussion (and even publication) of its documents, it was definitely acting as a force for good—against repression. Some of the actions early in the Arab Spring [pro-democracy rebellions in the Middle East from December 2010 into the spring of 2011]—aimed against the websites of governments trying to suppress citizens—were arguably useful (though it's hard to evaluate their real impact).

Moving Out of Credit

Attacking PayPal and MasterCard, though, was less smart, even if it was principled (the principle being that Anonymous likes WikiLeaks, and PayPal and MasterCard were doing things that didn't help WikiLeaks, so Anonymous would be unhelpful in return). The flaw, though, was that many people were recruited to allow their PCs [personal computers] to be used as bots in botnets[4] targeting those sites using the LOIC[5] software. The problem with that is that knowingly being part of a

---

4. A botnet refers to a collection of compromised computers running programs such as worms, Trojan horses, or backdoors under a common command. A botnet's originator can control the group remotely and usually does so for nefarious purposes.

DDoS[6] attack is against the law in the US, UK and a number of other countries; arrests followed. The FBI [Federal Bureau of Investigation] is reportedly working through a list of a thousand IP [Internet protocol] addresses whose owners may face arrest; so far it's still in the first hundred or so.

Further down the defensibility scale was the attack on the website of ACS:Law. The London solicitors firm had already made a bad name for itself by sending out letters to people claiming that they had illicitly downloaded music or pornographic films, and that they could avoid a costly legal case by just stumping up a few hundred pounds. ACS:Law's site collapsed under Anonymous's attack, and spilt its guts—in the form of e-mails and internal details. Arguably, that hastened the end of the firm by embarrassing it terribly and bringing it into the spotlight; but the speed with which it capitulated in the court cases brought against it, and that its founder Andrew Crossley had already been investigated by the Solicitors Regulation Authority, might have had just as much to do with it. What's also definite is that huge amounts of personal data was leaked as a direct result of those attacks, and a significant amount was embarrassing, containing as it did ACS:Law's allegations of the names of people who had downloaded films— and the names of the films.

And similarly there was the hack by Anonymous (and including members of LulzSec) of HBGary, a US military contractor. HBGary came to the group's attention because Aaron Barr, its chief, decided to try to penetrate Anonymous.

Anonymous turned over HBGary, but nothing of any great value emerged—although there are plenty of nuggets amid the many e-mails, not least that there is a whole cadre of private

5. LOIC, Low Orbit Ion Cannon, is an open source denial-of-service attack application named after a fictitious weapon from the Command & Conquer series of video games.
6. DDoS, distributed denial-of-service, are electronic attacks involving multiple computers that send repeated requests to a site that overloads its server and thus renders it inaccessible for a period of time.

companies in the US which are setting themselves up to provide cyber-defence—or possibly attack—to the highest bidder.

But part of that hack also involved leaking personal details of HBGary staff, and threats against them. Ugly? Yes. Avoidable? Yes: It's very simple to obfuscate contact details—it's the work of two minutes using regex[7] to blank, say, all but the last four digits of a mobile or home number, or only the last four digits of a number. It proves that you've got it, but without the collateral damage of spreading it over the Net. Certainly there's nothing to be gained from posting the full details of people who had entered competitions on the *Sun*'s site; yet they were splattered over Pastebin.

Rules of Engagement

Perhaps Anonymous needs to figure out some rules of engagement, because it's actually starting to repel some of the people who thought they liked its ideas; that's clear from what we might call the "Not so dear John Doe" letters on Pastebin.

All that seems to be left, as a result, is a few hacking crews, who seem to be of an age which doesn't yield that much wisdom: Folks such as TeamPoison and his disappointing grade in Computer Science AS-level [a British public examination to determine qualification in a particular course content]; or another (we're fairly sure) British-based hacking crew who would like to emulate LulzSec, and have spent the past week or so hacking and DDoSing (unwisely, I think) various government, police and military sites in the US and UK. (I'm not going to name them, because it only encourages them.)

OK, so it's hacking, and it seems like fun, at least until the police come knocking on your door. But for Anonymous, which for a while entertained the idea that it could be so much more, the past couple of months have seemed like the downward arc from something that seemed promising to

7. Regex, short for regular expression, here refers to the process of using software to recognize a pattern in phone numbers and then block them out.

something that is just a mess. Cyberactivism? Well, perhaps if you subtract the "activism" part. As one well-publicised tweet says, you can't arrest an idea. But you can certainly corrupt it.

> *"Each round of conflict [over Internet freedom] draws in additional supporters ... who believe, more and more, that the radical openness of the Web should set the pattern for everything."*

Some Activist Hackers Oppose Corporate Control of the Internet

Tim Hwang

In the following viewpoint, Tim Hwang asserts that since the Internet's inception, people have been embroiled in an ideological war over how it should be shaped. Some believe that the Internet should support existing institutions, while others believe it should be open and transparent, he maintains. Indeed, Hwang argues, 2011 hacker attacks in support of WikiLeaks, an organization that publishes secret documents, reflect a tradition of battles such as the fight for open-source software and peer-to-peer file sharing. While some believe that the Internet will succumb to control, those committed to Internet freedom are legion and willing to fight. Hwang, a former researcher at Harvard's Berkman Center for Internet & Society, founded ROFLCon, an Internet culture conference.

As you read, consider the following questions:

1. To what other "Long War" does Hwang compare the war over Internet control?

2. What does the author claim is one of the first battles between hackers and institutions?

3. Who does the author claim are the antagonists in the battle over copyright law?

Some historians like to talk about the "Long War" of the 20th century, a conflict spanning both world wars and the wars in Korea and Vietnam. They stress that this Long War was a single struggle over what kind of political system would rule the world—democracy, communism or fascism—and that what a war is fought over is often more important than the specifics of individual armies and nations.

Two Sides in a Long War

The Internet, too, is embroiled in a Long War.

The latest fighters on one side are Julian Assange, founder of WikiLeaks[1], and the media-dubbed "hacker army" that has risen in his defense in the past week [early December 2010], staging coordinated attacks on government and corporate institutions that have stood in his way. They come from a long tradition of Internet expansionists, who hold that the Web should remake the rest of the world in its own image. They believe that decentralized, transparent and radically open networks should be the organizing principle for all things in society, big and small.

On the other side are those who believe fundamentally that the world should remake the Web in its own image. This

---

1. WikiLeaks publishes documents otherwise unavailable to the public from anonymous sources whose identity is protected. A wiki allows any user to add or edit content, but the site now follows a more traditional publishing model, accepting submissions that are vetted by staff members and volunteers from mainstream news media.

side believes that the Internet at its heart is simply a tool, something that should be shaped to serve the demands of existing institutions. Each side seeks to mold the technology and standards of the Web to suit its particular vision.

In this current conflict, the loose confederation of "hacktivists" who rallied in support of Assange in what they called Operation Payback, targeted MasterCard, PayPal, Visa and other companies with a denial-of-service attack effectively preventing Web sites from operating. It's a global effort of often surprising scope; Dutch police said they arrested a 16-year-old last week suspected to be involved.

Their cause, from which Assange has publicly distanced himself, follows the simple logic of independence. One self-declared spokesperson for the "Anonymous" group doing battle for WikiLeaks explained its philosophy to the *Guardian* newspaper.

"We're against corporations and government interfering on the Internet," said the 22-year-old, identified only as Coldblood. "We believe it should be open and free for everyone."

Not the First Battle

The battle between "Anonymous" and the establishment isn't the first in the Long War between media-dubbed "hackers" and institutions, and considering the conflict's progression is key to understanding where it will lead.

In the early 1980s, Richard Stallman, then an employee at MIT's [Massachusetts Institute of Technology's] artificial-intelligence lab, was denied permission to access and edit computer code for the lab's laser printer. Frustrated, he kicked off what he calls GNU, a massively collaborative project to create a free and sharable operating system. His efforts sparked a widespread movement challenging the restriction of access to software through patents. Supporters asserted that they had a right to control the code in their own computers.

The Value of the Open-Source World

When key software technologies are developed in a closed-source, corporate environment, the negotiating power of marginalized social groups and users is sufficiently diminished. Various forms of resistance and counter-mobilization may appear, and may even have significant impact, but these reactive efforts are constrained by the technical codes built into the technologies by those in power. In the open-source world, actors have one more degree of freedom, allowing for the proactive shaping and modification of technologies, both in design and use. While this degree of freedom can also be used and abused by dominant interests, there is little question that the open-source approach allows greater latitude in challenging hegemony.

Brent K. Jesiek,
"Democratizing Software: Open Source, the Hacker Ethic,
and Beyond," First Monday, vol. 8, no. 3, October 6, 2003.

The battle reached far beyond Stallman, eventually pitting corporations and patent holders against this early generation of free-software advocates. The bulk of most software is still private, though open-source projects have gained popularity and even dominance in some arenas. Stallman continues to advocate for free software.

Another major milestone in the conflict arose in 1999, when Shawn Fanning launched Napster, allowing for seamless peer-to-peer sharing of content. The service ballooned, claiming more than 25 million users at its peak and resulting in mountains of copyrighted content flowing freely across the Web. The site was sued and shut down in 2001. However, the ensuing battle over copyright law drew a line between industry representatives, such as the Recording Industry Association of America, and the "hacker" advocates for the free flow of content.

Though Napster was forced to stop operating as a free service, the culture and innovation that it launched continued to grow. This led to the creation in 2001 of BitTorrent, a distributed and difficult-to-track peer-to-peer method of transferring large files.

Large-scale use of this technology emerged in 2003 in the form of the Pirate Bay, which indexes BitTorrent[2] files en masse. The site's founders and operators, Gottfrid Svartholm Warg, Carl Lundström, Fredrik Neij and Peter Sunde, would emerge as the Assanges of this battle, permitting a massive and continuous leak of copyrighted content in the face of waves of police raids and lawsuits—persisting even beyond their eventual conviction on infringement charges in 2009.

The WikiLeaks fight is in the tradition of these conflicts, just on a much vaster scale. As the Internet has become an integral part of our everyday lives, narrow and technical questions about who gets to run and edit computer code have morphed first into battles over copyrighted content, and now into fights at the highest levels of government secrecy and corporate power. Assange's efforts to undermine the secrecy and control of established institutions—and the attacks his defenders have launched against MasterCard, a Swedish prosecutor and possibly Sarah Palin's political action committee— are the latest and highest form of a war that has been waged for decades.

Who Will Control the Web?

So what is the future of this Long War?

In his recent book *The Master Switch*, Columbia law professor Tim Wu makes the case that the Internet, on its most

---

2. BitTorrent is a peer-to-peer (P2P) communications protocol for the sharing of files, here copyrighted content such as music and movies.

basic level, is just like any other communications medium. As such, we shouldn't be surprised to see consolidation and government control over the Web. It's true that most other media—movies, radio and television—have gone through phases of wild growth and experimentation, eventually settling into a pattern of consolidation and control.

Why should we expect any different of the Web? Is the arc of the Internet's Long War predetermined?

One key factor is embedded in the history of the Web and the many iterations of the Long War itself: The Internet has cultivated a public vested in its freedom. Each round of conflict draws in additional supporters, from hackers to the growing numbers of open-government activists and everyday users who believe, more and more, that the radical openness of the Web should set the pattern for everything.

As the battlefield has become more vast—from laser printer code to transparency in global diplomacy—the Internet's standing army continues to grow and is spoiling for a fight.

"*In response to China's crackdown [on Internet freedom], and to restrictions in many Middle Eastern countries as well, a small army has been mustered to defeat them. 'Hacktivists,' they call themselves.*"

Great Firewall: Chinese Censors of Internet Face "Hacktivists" in U.S.

Geoffrey Fowler

In the following viewpoint, Wall Street Journal *technical reporter Geoffrey Fowler maintains that some hack the Internet to oppose censorship in repressive nations. Fowler tells the story of Bill Xia, whose Freegate program helps people gain access to information that the Chinese government does not want its citizens to see. Monitoring the program takes constant vigilance and communication with a team of volunteer programmers, the author claims. Indeed, Fowler asserts, China did on one occasion block Mr. Xia's site, although he has since overcome the problem. Although plenty of Chinese Internet users are not interested in free speech or government repression, many appreciate learning the truth about issues that affect them.*

As you read, consider the following questions:

1. How does Fowler describe the activities of what is often called the Great Firewall of China?

2. How does Susan Stevens describe her "adopt a blog" program?

3. According to the author, how did one twenty-two-year-old who works in Chinese media describe the limits of Freegate?

Surfing the Web last fall a Chinese high-school student who calls himself Zivn noticed something missing. It was Wikipedia, an online encyclopedia that accepts contributions or edits from users, and that he himself had contributed to.

The Chinese government, in October, had added Wikipedia to a list of Web sites and phrases it blocks from Internet users. For Zivn, trying to surf this and many other Web sites, including the BBC's Chinese-language news service, brought just an error message. But the 17-year-old had loved the way those sites helped him put China's official pronouncements in perspective. "There were so many lies among the facts, and I could not find where the truth is," he writes in an instant-message interview.

Then some friends told him where to find Freegate, a software program that thwarts the Chinese government's vast system to limit what its citizens see. Freegate—by connecting computers inside of China to servers in the U.S.—enables Zivn and others to keep reading and writing to Wikipedia and countless other Web sites.

Behind Freegate is a North Carolina–based Chinese hacker named Bill Xia. He calls it his red pill, a reference to the drug in *The Matrix* movies that vaulted unconscious captives of a totalitarian regime into the real world. Mr. Xia likes to refer to the villainous Agent Smith from *The Matrix* films, noting that the digital bad guy in sunglasses "guards the Matrix like China's Public Security Bureau guards the Internet."

Roughly a dozen Chinese government agencies employ thousands of Web censors, Internet cafe police and computers that constantly screen traffic for forbidden content and sources—a barrier often called the Great Firewall of China. Type, say, "media censorship by China" into e-mails, chats or Web logs, and the messages never arrive.

Even with this extensive censorship, Chinese are getting vast amounts of information electronically that they never would have found a decade ago. The growth of the Internet in China—to an estimated 111 million users—was one reason the authorities, after a week's silence, ultimately had to acknowledge a disastrous toxic spill in a river late last year. But the government recently has redoubled its efforts to narrow the Net's reach on sensitive matters.

It has required all bloggers, or writers of Web logs, to register. At the end of last year, 15 Internet writers were in jail in China, according to the Committee to Protect Journalists, a New York group. China also has gotten some U.S. Internet companies to limit the search results they provide or the discussions they host on their Chinese services. A tiny firm Mr. Xia set up to provide and maintain Freegate had to lobby computer-security companies such as Symantec Corp., of Cupertino, Calif., not to treat it as a virus.

In response to China's crackdown, and to restrictions in many Middle Eastern countries as well, a small army has been mustered to defeat them. "Hacktivists," they call themselves.

Bennett Haselton, a security consultant and former Microsoft programmer, has developed a system called the Circumventor. It connects volunteers around the world with Web users in China and the Middle East so they can use their hosts' personal computers to read forbidden sites.

Susan Stevens, a Las Vegas graphic designer, belongs to an "adopt a blog" program. She has adopted a Chinese blogger by using her own server in the U.S. to broadcast his very personal musings on religion to the world. She has never left the U.S., but "this is where technology excels," she says. "We don't have to have anything in common. We barely have to speak the same language."

In Boston, computer scientist Roger Dingledine tends to Tor, a modified version of a U.S. Naval Research Laboratory project, which disguises the identities of Chinese Web surfers by sending messages through several layers of hosts to obscure their path. In addition to the Department of Defense, Mr. Dingledine had also received funding from the Electronic Frontier Foundation, a nonprofit group that supports free speech online.

Freegate has advantages over some of its peers. As the product of ethnically Chinese programmers, it uses the language and fits the culture. It is a simple and small program, whose file size of just 137 kilobytes helps make it easy to store in an e-mail program and pass along on a portable memory drive.

Mr. Xia says about 100,000 users a day use Freegate or two other censorship-defeating systems he helped to create. It is impossible to confirm that claim, but Freegate and similar programs from others, called UltraReach and Garden Networks, are becoming a part of the surfing habits of China's Internet elite in universities, cafes and newsrooms.

Freegate has a big booster in Falun Gong, the spiritual group China banned in 1999 as subversive. It is a practice of meditations and breathing exercises based on moralistic teachings by its founder, Li Hongzhi. Chinese expatriates—marrying U.S. free-speech politics with protests over persecution of Falun Gong practitioners in China—have focused their energy on breaking China's censorship systems. They have nurtured the work of Mr. Xia, himself a Falun Gong follower, and several other programmers.

Copyright © 2010, by Monte Wolverton and CagleCartoons.com.

Freegate also gets a financial boost from the U.S. government. Voice of America and Radio Free Asia, part of the federal government's Broadcasting Board of Governors, pay Mr. Xia and others to send out e-mails featuring links to their stories.

Kenneth Berman, manager of the anticensorship office of the board's International Broadcasting Bureau, declines to say how much it compensates Mr. Xia's company. He says the bureau pays less than $5 million a year to companies to help combat Internet censorship abroad, especially in China and Iran.

"Our policy is to allow individuals to get anything they want, when they want," Mr. Berman says. "Bill and his techniques help us do that."

Human Rights in China, a New York nonprofit group funded by individuals and charities founded by Chinese scientists and scholars in 1989, also helps fund Mr. Xia's enterprise, which runs on a budget of about $1 million a year, and pays it to send out e-mails.

The resources behind Freegate and other hacktivists could increase if Congress revives a bill to create an Office of Global Internet Freedom. U.S. Internet companies have drawn strong criticism in Congress for compliance with Chinese Web restriction, and hearings on their activities are set for Wednesday. Microsoft Corp., Redmond, Wash.; Google Inc., Mountain View, Calif.; and Yahoo Inc., Sunnyvale, Calif., all say that they abide by local laws. Microsoft's general counsel said this month that the software giant shuts down personal blogs only if it receives a "legally binding notice from a government."

Several Chinese agencies with jurisdiction over the Internet, including the Ministries of Public Security, State Security, and Information Industry, didn't respond to faxed questions about Internet filtering. The State Council Information Office said the government would hold a news conference to address "Internet security" issues early this week. It didn't respond to specific questions. A position paper issued in 2000 by the National People's Congress said it is a criminal offense to use the Internet to "incite subversion," to "divulge state secrets" or to "organize cults." The paper said the laws were needed "to promote the good and eliminate the bad, encourage the healthy development of the Internet [and] safeguard the security of the State and the public interest."

It is this attitude that drives Mr. Xia's counterattack. Moving to the U.S. a decade ago to begin graduate studies in physics, he says, he never imagined becoming either a dissident or a programmer. Slowly, he became more uncomfortable with China's restriction of public discourse. In the U.S., he watched taped footage of the 1989 Tiananmen Square assault on protesters.

Mr. Xia says he taught himself computer science out of textbooks and in 2002 set up a small company called Dynamic Internet Technology Inc., hiring 10 people to help send out e-mails for such clients as Voice of America. He says he takes no salary, living a modest life off his savings and his wife's earnings.

Often working alone at his computer until 3 a.m., Mr. Xia lives like a secret agent, communicating with a small team of volunteer programmers across North America over secure e-mail or coded phone calls. He combs his house with a device to detect the loose radio waves of bugging devices. In his 30s, Mr. Xia asked that the city in which he lives and works not be disclosed so he can maintain a low profile.

The programmer says he dashes to his computer as soon as he wakes up each morning, to make sure his system is still intact. He keeps a raft of programs running on his oversize flat-screen monitor, testing Freegate through a dozen different Web browsers and instant-message and chat programs.

Freegate works by constantly changing the address of its U.S. servers so that China can't block the connection, and users like Zivn, the 17-year-old, can read and write at will. Zivn says he uses Freegate three to four times a week to read domestic and international news. Besides the BBC site, he frequents Radio Free Asia and the *Epoch Times*, a newspaper that champions Falun Gong. All have Chinese-language news services normally blocked by China's firewall.

Zivn says he isn't a member of Falun Gong and describes his political slant as "neutral." He says he has read about North Korean leader Kim Jong-il's recent secret visit to China and the closure of a liberal Chinese magazine called *Freezing Point*. He says he has copied some foreign news reports onto his personal blog, which is available inside China and periodically gets blocked itself.

One user, who describes himself online as a 22-year-old who works in Chinese media, praises the software but adds that its use is "limited to a small group of people who are knowledgeable about computers and the Internet." Most Chinese, he says, "have not realized the harmful effects from network blocking." China's Internet control system, called Golden Shield, doesn't aim for complete control over information but rather to discover and plug major breaches in the firewall.

Nor can Freegate prevent self-censorship. Many Chinese surfers and bloggers, having a sense of the forbidden words and topics, check themselves before they cross the line.

Then, too, many Chinese are as frivolous in their Internet use as anyone else. Most of China's estimated 33 million bloggers write about entertainment, fashion and such, not the free-speech or police crackdowns. Still, Mr. Xia says he sees a rise in Freegate traffic after events such as democracy protests or corruption scandals, which the state-controlled press doesn't cover.

Freegate's Web site supports an effort by Falun Gong's *Epoch Times* to get Chinese citizens who belong to the Communist Party to renounce their membership, and the paper claims nearly eight million have signed a petition doing so. Many did so through Freegate, Mr. Xia says.

Mr. Xia says he gets a mountain of feedback. He convinced Symantec not to treat Freegate as a virus. "The users are not technical. They just say, 'It doesn't work!' and we have to ask them a lot of questions" to resolve problems, Mr. Xia says. He politely declines the help of volunteers inside China, fearing that they might be government spies or that they would be punished if discovered.

Occasionally, he says, he gets tips from Chinese who say they have been given the job of maintaining the Internet restrictions. "One guy told us, 'Sorry, I participated in some efforts to block your software. I think it is not going to work in a few days,'" Mr. Xia says. "China may have many people working on the firewall, but for them it is just a job."

When Mr. Xia got into this work, the anticensorship movement's great hope at that time was dying. It was a program called Triangle Boy, which worked by connecting Chinese users to a regularly updated list of secret portals, called proxy servers, hosted overseas. It worked well until 2002, when China sped up its countering system to close those holes in its firewall within hours after noticing a leak. Short of resources and solutions, Triangle Boy couldn't keep up.

Similarly, with each new version of Freegate—now on its sixth release—the censors "just keep improving and adding more manpower to monitor what we have been doing," Mr. Xia says. In turn, he and volunteer programmers keep tweaking Freegate.

At first, the software automatically changed its Internet protocol address—a sort of phone number for a Web site— faster than China could block it. That worked until September 2002, when China blocked Freegate's domain name, not just its number, in the Internet phone book.

The government accomplished that by actually taking over China's whole portion of the Internet naming system, the common directory that computers on the Internet use to talk with each other. It then diverted Freegate users from the company's North American servers to several addresses China had picked.

More than three years later, Mr. Xia still is amazed by the bold move, calling it a "hijacking." Ultimately he prevailed, through a solution he won't identify for fear of being shut down for good.

Confident in that fix, Mr. Xia continues to send out his red pill, and users like Zivn continue to take it. The teen credits his cultural and political perspective to a "generation gap" that has come of having access to more information. "I am just gradually getting used to the truth about the real world," he writes.

Periodical and Internet Sources Bibliography

The following articles have been selected to supplement the diverse views presented in this chapter.

Derek E. Bambauer and Oliver Day	"The Hacker's Aegis," Brooklyn Law School, Legal Studies Paper, no. 184, March 1, 2010.
Marcia Clemmitt	"Computer Hacking," *CQ Researcher*, September 16, 2011.
Economist	"Cybercrime: Black Hats, Grey Hairs," August 6, 2011.
Michael Joseph Gross	"Enter the Cyber-Dragon," *Vanity Fair*, September 2011.
PC Quest	"Hacktivists: A New Breed of Cybercriminals," October 2011.
Andrew S. Ross	"Free-Speech Advocates Silent on BART Hacking," *San Francisco Chronicle*, August 16, 2011.
Yasmine Ryan	"Anonymous and the Arab Uprisings," Al Jazeera, May 19, 2011. www.aljazeera.com.
Gerry Smith	"DefCon: Hacker Conference Exposes Lax Security of Companies, Other Hackers," *Huffington Post*, August 6, 2011. www.huffingtonpost.com.
Jason Tanz	"Kinect Hackers Are Changing the Future of Robotics," *Wired*, July 2011.
Robert Vamosi	"How Hacktivism Affects Us All," *PCWorld*, September 2011.
Ashlee Vance and Miguel Helft	"Hackers Give Web Companies a Test of Free Speech," *New York Times*, December 8, 2010.

OPPOSING
VIEWPOINTS®
SERIES

CHAPTER 4

What Laws Will Best Prevent Cybercrime?

Chapter Preface

One of several controversies in the debate over what laws will best prevent cybercrime is whether the government has in fact done enough to protect its own computer infrastructure. While some laud the government's efforts, other analysts argue that the government has failed to solve the nation's cybersecurity problems. "We know how we can be penetrated," claims Senator Benjamin L. Cardin, chair of the Senate Judiciary Committee's Subcommittee on Terrorism and Homeland Security. However, he concedes, "We don't know how to prevent it effectively."

Since 1984, when Congress passed the Counterfeit Access Device and Computer Fraud and Abuse Act—the first law designed to address computer security—the US government has been trying to establish laws, policies, and practices to combat cybercrime and protect American institutions. Following the terrorist attacks of September 11, 2001, Congress passed the Cybersecurity Enhancement Act to expand the powers of law enforcement to prosecute computer crimes. In 2003 the George W. Bush administration issued Homeland Security Presidential Directive 7, which gave the Department of Homeland Security (DHS) the task of protecting nonmilitary cyberspace infrastructure. President Barack Obama commissioned a report to analyze the effectiveness of cyberspace policy shortly after he took office. The news was not good. Indeed, the May 2009 "Cyberspace Policy Review: Assuring a Trusted and Resilient Information and Communications Infrastructure" confirmed fears that "the nation's approach to cybersecurity over the past 15 years has failed to keep pace with the threat."

One flaw cited by the report was an ineffective organizational structure. "Responsibilities for cybersecurity are distributed across a wide array of federal departments and agencies, many with overlapping authorities, and none with sufficient decision authority to direct actions that deal with often conflicting issues in a consistent way." In response, the DHS launched efforts to coordinate a National Cyber Incident Response Plan (NCIRP) to address these concerns. In September 2010, DHS tested this plan in Cyber Storm III, a series of cyber-defense exercises. Following these exercises, the DHS concluded that NCIRP provides a good framework and shows improvement in collaboration. However, its July 2011 report indicates that clarification of roles and standard and complementary operation procedures across agencies are necessary.

Some commentators claim that putting cybersecurity in the hands of the DHS is poor policy. Amit Yoran, chief executive officer of the network management and security company NetWitness Corp., asserts, "While pockets of progress have been made, administrative incompetence and political infighting have squandered meaningful progress and for years now our adversaries continue to aggressively press their advantage." Other analysts claim that security agencies must change how they think about cybersecurity. These critics argue that the United States cannot defend against cyber attacks the same way it defends against traditional attacks. According to Naval Postgraduate School professor John Arquilla, "Our paradigm is a firewall-based, Maginot Line[1] mentality." Building walls against cyber attacks is inadequate, he claims: "As any good hacker will tell you, there are no firewalls. The master hackers walk through these firewalls the way you and I walk through a room." Arquilla believes that more encryption is the key. "We're a vastly under-encrypted society and military. The only way to provide some reasonable modicum of security is to recognize that the bad boys will always get in, and so you have

---

1. The Maginot Line was a series of fixed bunkers and armed forts along the border with Germany that the French built to ward off invasion. However, Germany ultimately defeated France by first invading Belgium and going around the wall. The wall of defenses was also very costly for the French. Thus, the Maginot Line has come to represent costly, old-fashioned thinking when evaluating defense options.

to encrypt, encrypt, encrypt so that they don't know what they have when they do get in."

Whether the government is up to the challenge of cyber defense continues to be contested by the critics. The authors in the following chapter present their views on which laws will best prevent cybercrime. That Congress sees the need for increased cybersecurity to protect America is clear; how to do so is less clear. Nevertheless, claims security specialist Kevin Coleman, "In the years I've been on this Earth, I've never seen Capitol Hill in such agreement on the need to fix this."

"A comprehensive federal data breach law ... should do more to encourage data collection and retention practices that reduce the risk of breaches in the first place."

A Strict National Standard Is Necessary to Encourage Companies to Disclose Data Breaches

Andrew Crocker

Studies show that data breaches, in which companies release personal information from databases without permission, are a continuing problem, asserts Andrew Crocker in the following viewpoint. Unfortunately, he maintains, federal laws require consumer notification under limited circumstances. Moreover, Crocker claims, states have their own notification laws, making it difficult for companies to know when they should notify consumers. Thus, Crocker argues, a federal law that standardizes existing laws is needed. Crocker, a Harvard University law student, has worked at the Berkman Center for Internet & Society and as editor for Harvard's Journal of Law and Technology.

As you read, consider the following questions:

1. According to Crocker, how should the range of sensitive data in the security requirements of federal laws be expanded?

2. How does the author explain the difference between a "notify unless" and a "notify if" standard?

3. In the author's opinion, what do the Bono Mack, Rush, and Pryor/Rockefeller bills require of businesses in addition to providing notice of a data breach?

This summer [2011], the number of data breaches at high-profile companies rivals only the surge in temperature. But despite the newfound attention, data breaches aren't new; according to the Privacy Rights Clearinghouse, since 2005 there have been nearly 2600 data breaches affecting over 500 million records.

Meanwhile, the legal picture surrounding breaches is complex. Current federal law requires notification of consumers in the event of a breach only in limited circumstances, while nearly every state has its own version of a data breach law. Congress is now looking to simplify data breach laws with a national standard, but the question is whether such a standard would be a step forward for consumers. It's an issue, that CDT [Center for Democracy & Technology] has been following since at least 2005.

Comparing Data Breach Proposals

At present, there are a number of pending data breach bills, including Representative [Bobby] Rush's DATA [Data Accountability and Trust Act], Representative [Mary] Bono Mack's recently marked up SAFE Data Act, and Senators [Mark] Pryor and [Jay] Rockefeller's (acronym-free) Data Security and Breach Notification Act. Other pending legislation, including

Senator [Patrick] Leahy's Personal Data Privacy and Security Act as well as the White House's Cybersecurity Proposal, also addresses data breaches.[1]

CDT believes a comprehensive federal data breach law would be useful to standardize existing laws, but above all, the law should do more to encourage data collection and retention practices that reduce the risk of breaches in the first place. Certainly, a new federal law should not weaken existing notification and security requirements already in place today under state law and the FTC [Federal Trade Commission] Act. Current congressional bills differ slightly on their approach to protecting consumer data from security breach. Below is a comparison of a few key provisions:

• *Information Security Requirements*: The bills proposed by Representative Bono Mack, Representative Rush, and Senators Pryor and Rockefeller would empower the FTC to promulgate regulations for businesses' handling of personal data. These would include appointing information security managers, identifying and correcting potential data security vulnerabilities, and taking steps to safely dispose of electronic personal data. The Rush, Pryor/Rockefeller, and Leahy bills also would make so-called information brokers, businesses that compile databases of thousands of consumers' data and sell this information to third parties, subject to special requirements— which CDT supports—that ensure the data they compile is accurate and that consumers have access to this data and the ability to dispute inaccuracies. Representative Bono Mack's bill adds a requirement for data minimization, so that a business retains only data needed for a legitimate business purpose and otherwise disposes of personal information as soon as pos-

---

1. As of this writing, Rush's Data Accountability and Trust Act, H.R. 1707; Mack's SAFE Data Act, H.R. 2477; and Pryor and Rockefeller's Data Security and Breach Notification Act, S. 1207, have been referred to committee. Leahy's Personal Data Privacy and Security Act, S. 1151, was reported by committee on September 22, 2011.

sible. CDT supports these information security provisions, particularly in combination with a data minimization provision.

CDT would like to see the bills incorporate a broader range of sensitive data into the security requirements. The bills' definition of "personal information" applies to both breach notification and security, but CDT believes companies should be under some explicit obligation to protect personal data that is not sensitive enough to require notification in the event of a breach. This would be consistent with the Federal Trade Commission's (FTC) implementation of the security requirements of Gramm-Leach-Bliley[2]—the FTC requires safeguards for essentially "any record containing nonpublic personal information" about a customer. The FTC [Act], under its section 5 authority to curb unfair business practices, also requires reasonable security to prevent unauthorized access to nonpublic, nonfinancial data—as demonstrated by the FTC's 2010 complaint against Twitter.

Notification Requirements

• *Notification Trigger*: Of course, even the best security practices will not prevent all data breaches. In the event of a breach, the bills generally require notification of all individuals affected. However, the bills also exempt businesses from notification if they perform a risk assessment that determines there is no "reasonable" or "significant" risk, of harm, such as identity fraud. In addition, use of FTC-approved encryption technologies creates a rebuttable presumption that there is no reasonable risk of harm, unless the encryption key has also been breached. CDT supports a "notify unless" standard of reasonable risk, meaning that a business must notify consum-

2. In addition to allowing commercial banks, investment banks, securities firms, and insurance companies to consolidate, the Gramm-Leach-Bliley Act required that financial institutions have a policy in place to protect personal information from foreseeable threats in security and data integrity, as well as establish rules to govern the collection and disclosure of that information.

ers unless an affirmative determination of no risk can be made. This is in contrast to a "notify if" standard, requiring an affirmative finding of risk for notification, which would create an incentive for companies not to fully investigate data breaches. Many of the bills now take this approach, but it remains possible that the presumption could be reversed by seemingly minor language changes as the legislative process moves forward.

Senator Leahy's bill and the White House proposal include an additional valuable requirement that if a business makes an affirmative determination of no risk, it is still required to promptly inform the government of this result. CDT supports this provision because companies are more likely to make good faith, honest risk appraisals when those appraisals will be filed with the government.

Looking at Similarities and Differences

• *Information Covered*: Each bills differs slightly in its definition of "personal information." In general, covered personal information includes an individual's first name or initial and last name, in combination with other forms of identifying information, such as address, Social Security number, driver's license, or financial account information. The Leahy bill would also cover unique biometric data, an important category of personally identifiable information. CDT supports including health data under a breach notification, with authority for the FTC to modify the covered categories through rule making.

• *Consumer Assistance*: In addition to the standard notification to individuals whose information has been breached, the Bono Mack, Rush, and Pryor/Rockefeller bills would require businesses to offer two years of credit monitoring services at no cost to the individual.

• *Preemption of State Law*: All of the current bills would supersede state data breach notification laws, although the Rush and Rockefeller/Pryor bills would make exceptions for state victim assistance requirements. Preempting state laws may be necessary to simplify businesses' obligations, but CDT cautions that the federal regime should therefore not be weaker than current state laws. In addition, the legislation should not preempt all state data security laws, only those that cover the same information covered in the legislation, so that states are able to add data security requirements to other categories of data that are not covered by the legislation.

Ideally, legislation addressing data security and data breaches would be incorporated into broader, baseline consumer privacy legislation. If Congress elects to pursue data breach notification independently, however, it should take care not to weaken the notification regime currently in place at the state level. CDT hopes that Congress continues to refine these bills and ultimately enacts meaningful protections that offer concrete improvements in data security.

> "Self-regulation [to protect consumers from data attacks] is far preferable to government control."

Industry Self-Regulation, Not Government Intervention, Is the Best Way to Protect Consumers from Data Attacks

William H. Saito

In the following viewpoint, William H. Saito argues that to avoid harsh federal laws that limit consumer choice and hinder product development, businesses should take strong steps to protect personal data. Many consumers are unaware of the hidden vulnerabilities of modern technologies that put their personal information at risk, he maintains. Therefore, businesses must establish policies that inform consumers of vulnerabilities, make secure design a priority, and set high security standards, Saito claims. Lawmakers are not often technically sophisticated and overact to fears of technology, he reasons; thus self-regulation is the better alternative. Saito is an entrepreneur, venture capitalist, educator, and advisor on security issues worldwide.

William H. Saito, "Our Naked Data," *Futurist*, vol. 45, no. 4, July/August 2011, pp. 43–45. Copyright © 2011 by Futurist. All rights reserved. Reproduced by permission.

As you read, consider the following questions:

1. What did a 2010 Unisys Corporation survey reveal about American attitudes toward cell phone security?

2. What does Saito claim most technology companies are more concerned with than security?

3. In the author's view, what needs to be done concerning sensor data that contains personal information?

Many of us find ourselves with multiple gadgets—in our pockets, our homes, our cars, our offices—and these gadgets are increasingly built to talk to each other, often automatically and invisibly. Camera phones upload straight to the Web and connect through WiFi and Bluetooth to unseen computer networks; the printer next to your desk can suddenly start printing out documents sent from a branch office on the other side of the world, and our cars automatically pull down information from the sky on the latest traffic and weather conditions.

The Risks of Convenience

A 2010 survey by Unisys Corporation showed that most Americans are largely unaware of the threat posed by data vulnerability. For instance, while a majority (73%) of Americans said they regularly update the computer virus detection software on their home computers, only a minority (37%) said they updated their cell phone passwords regularly, and nearly the same portion (36%) do not update mobile passwords at all.

Even common documents (licenses, passports, payment cards) that we carry around with us contain RFID [radio-frequency identification] chips. All these sensors and transmitters are constantly busy, silently collecting and giving away our personal information to other devices, often without our knowledge. Every time such information is transmitted and received, there is a very real risk that the data may be intercepted by people other than those for whom it was originally intended, and tampered with or abused for criminal, terrorist, or other purposes.

Scientists actually may be more at risk than the average population, especially those in academic circles. For all the theoretical discussion of computer security, those inside the academic environment often do not take real security issues as seriously as do those in the business world. This indifference puts researchers at risk with regard to their data, especially those who are involved in research with potential commercial applications.

Scientists working on politically controversial or emotionally charged projects have also famously found themselves targets for security attacks: In 2010, the e-mail accounts of climate researchers from East Anglia University were hacked by conservative activists, who then attempted to use private messages to discredit the researchers academically and professionally. The researchers were subsequently cleared of any wrongdoing or impropriety, but their exoneration received much less public attention than the initial scandal.

The Global Positioning System

Numerous types of sensors were designed for our convenience, usually not with security in mind. By the end of 2010, almost 80% of cell phones had a built-in global positioning system (GPS) device, according to iSuppli. That's up from about 50% in 2009. These devices can be used to send information on the user's whereabouts to another place. For the most part, we see such technology as a welcome innovation, helping us find the nearest coffee shop when we are in a strange city, for example, or discover which of our friends is close at hand, thanks to social media applications.

We may have the option of allowing such information to be transmitted or of blocking it when we first start to use the application, but there are other ways of tracking phones (and people) without our consent or knowledge. The phone network is not the only system that provides information on our whereabouts; many digital cameras now also include GPS receivers, permitting the automatic geotagging of photos—i.e., instantly identifying the photographer's real-time location. Most modern cars are equipped with satellite navigation systems, which also transmit location information.

Backdoors

Our computer systems at home and at work are obvious security targets, but the existence of "backdoors"—methods for bypassing normal authentication—may not be that obvious. Networking over the air (WiFi) or over power lines and the use of Bluetooth gadgets help to reduce clutter and introduce flexibility, but they also introduce risk. "Free" wireless access points are sometimes set up to capture WiFi traffic, and it is now possible to spoof a global system for a mobile communications cellular tower to capture all cellular telephone calls in a specific targeted area. Clearly, politicians and celebrities are not immune to hacking, as seen by the recent revelations that members of the British press were routinely listening in on the voice mails of its citizens, including the royals.

To prevent channels between devices from being compromised, it is possible to encrypt the traffic; however, such encryption can slow down and impede users, and many "secure" products are quite vulnerable since the protocols are not well implemented. Often, the security and encryption on these devices is so troublesome to set up that many users (including corporate IT [information technology] departments) don't bother, or set things up incorrectly, falsely assuming they are protected.

Even if you're not using a wireless network or a Bluetooth keyboard, the electromagnetic emissions from the equipment you use can be monitored remotely, and in extreme cases may actually allow someone to read your screen through walls or from across the street.

You would think that most people by now would know something about the risks of viruses on their computers, yet many people happily download and install unknown applications from dubious sources, oblivious of the fact that their new software could hijack their PC's [personal computer's] camera and microphone and surreptitiously transmit audio and video to parties unknown. In fact, the simple microphones found in all laptops can be used to determine what keys are being typed on those keyboards.

Using Computer Peripherals

Misusing computer peripherals is sometimes an officially sanctioned activity, as shown in the case of the Pennsylvania school district that distributed student laptops with what the district termed "tracking security" features (but could better be described as Big Brother "spyware"), taking photographs of unsuspecting students in their homes.

While the proliferation of USB devices over the past few years has been a boon for computer users, it has also increased opportunities for data hacking. Small USB key loggers, similar in appearance to thumb drives or keyboard cable extenders, can remain undetected for months at a time, faithfully recording every password, confidential memo, and private thought before the device is retrieved (or the data automatically uploaded) and the contents analyzed, regardless of how tightly locked down your office's network is. Even innocent-seeming devices such as USB flash drives and CD-ROMs distributed at trade fairs, etc., can be used to install backdoors and "Trojan horses," sending confidential data such as banking passwords back to base, just as a "free" game downloaded to a mobile phone can open that device up to unlimited abuse.

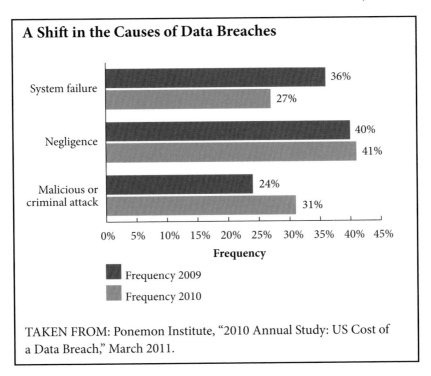

A Shift in the Causes of Data Breaches

TAKEN FROM: Ponemon Institute, "2010 Annual Study: US Cost of a Data Breach," March 2011.

Hidden Vulnerabilities

Nor, in case you're wondering, is the written word any more secure. Many office printers, copiers, and faxes now incorporate hard disks or other memory devices to capture, store, and transmit the printed and scanned images (we don't think of them as such, but modern copiers are actually sophisticated computers that can be easily compromised).

These memory devices are designed to be accessible for maintenance purposes: They can be removed and their contents read at leisure. The printouts and copies from many of these devices incorporate microscopic anticounterfeiting information, which can also be used for tracking purposes. And when you leave the building, all the smart cards and RFID chips that you carry around—the corporate entry cards, mass transit cards, passports, credit and debit cards, etc.—can also let people know who and where you are and what you're up to.

We can regard many of these security and privacy violations as essentially harmless, if irritating. Vending machines in Japanese train stations, for example, can automatically recommend drinks to customers based on their age, sex, and other factors. Annoying text messages may pop up on your cell phone, inviting you to enjoy a discounted latte every time you come within 100 yards of a coffee shop that you've visited in the past. But far more frightening are the criminals obtaining or abusing such information. The "safety blanket" supposedly provided by these RFID chips is an illusion, since the chips, together with their content, can be cloned, with all the attendant problems of identity theft.

A More Data-Secure World

Computer scientists both outside and inside the IT industry need to understand the essence of security and how the data that they collect will affect the overall system. The goal is to mitigate the risk of unintentional data leakage, which leads to other security issues. One way to do this is for researchers to find the flaws in the systems they use, but manufacturers seldom welcome these efforts.

A change in attitude needs to take place regarding the responsible disclosure of exploits by independent researchers: The discoveries need to be welcomed and acted upon, rather than seen as challenges to professional competence. Currently, there is a surprising lack of awareness of the risks posed by data breaches; the majority of technology companies are more concerned with (and devote large amounts of R&D [research and development] to) business continuity than with security.

As sensors become cheaper and more commonplace, the IT industry needs to take a consistent approach with regard to alerting consumers, at a user interface level, about the privacy risks resulting from the use of different sensors and applications, as well as a unified hardware and basic software approach to security. The emphasis on continuity rather than security illustrates that companies and organizations, including research institutions, need to take active security and privacy protection measures within their domains. The industry as a whole should be aware of the risks to their businesses posed by security breaches, and should take the necessary steps to guard against these risks.

Three Vital Steps

At least three steps are vitally necessary to head off what I see as a serious crisis developing—serious for individuals who will suffer as a result of abuses of their privacy and personal information, and also for the many companies and organizations that will suffer from all-too-predictable legislation enacted to protect citizens from the "evils" of technology being perverted by unscrupulous forces.

1. Inform the public of data products' vulnerabilities. The makers of all devices that are capable of collecting and/or transmitting data should inform the public of any known vulnerabilities associated with their products. Whether or not this should be a legal duty is another matter, as it is probably impossible for a company to come up with an exhaustive list of every way in which its products could be abused.

Industry, too, needs to create standardized guidelines on the use of sensor data that contains personal information. There needs to be a cross-industry "best practices" standard to govern the implementation of these sensors at the device level, which can be explained to end users in a standardized format so that the use of these is consistent.

2. Make security a data design priority. Companies engaged in such designing and manufacturing must proactively incorporate security in their products and the design process. Designers must balance the accelerated demand for new features against a possible regulatory backlash that may occur if security becomes a populist consumer issue.

There are real-world examples of how security is already being taken seriously in areas that may seem surprising. Some copier manufacturers, such as SHARP, offer and promote encryption on the hard drives built into their copiers and printers. Such encryption significantly reduces the value of a stolen or illegally accessed hard drive. Many laptop manufacturers now offer the option to disable USB ports (this is standard operating procedure in many corporate Windows desktop builds), and several cell phone manufacturers promote models without cameras. Unfortunately, these solutions fail to address the root cause of the issue; they are merely "patches" for a few of the holes in what is a veritable Swiss cheese of data *in*security.

3. Set high standards and enforce them. Perhaps most important of all, industry players must collaborate and implement stringent self-regulation to better define the collection and use of data from the different sensors in our lives. Moreover, global business must work closely with government to strengthen the penalties for any interception of information containing personal data not intended for the person or organization reading it.

We stand at a crossroads in terms of dealing with data security, and both paths are, for different reasons, highly unattractive. Prompt, meaningful self-regulation to avoid a coming crisis seems just as impossibly difficult to some as suffering the painful, throw-out-the-babies-with-the-bathwater overreaction of technically unsophisticated, politically motivated government regulators.

I argue that self-regulation is far preferable to government control. I am aware that cross-industry cooperation, not to mention industry-government cooperation, is no easy matter, but the consequences of delaying could be catastrophic. It is essential to avert this crisis so that consumer choice isn't restricted, manufacturers aren't shackled, and researchers aren't thwarted in their development work by a new wave of draconian personal-data protection laws.

| "Data retention is necessary to help track down and apprehend pedophiles who abuse children and destroy lives."

Laws to Protect Children from Internet Pornographers Are Necessary

Lamar Smith and Debbie Wasserman Schultz

The Internet makes it easy for online predators to distribute child pornography undetected, argue US representatives Lamar Smith and Debbie Wasserman Schultz in the following viewpoint. In fact, they claim, one of the only ways to find these predators is by tracking them on the Internet. Unfortunately, the authors maintain, by the time law enforcement have made a request, Internet service providers have often purged Internet address records. Thus, the authors assert, laws that require Internet service providers to retain data for longer periods so that law enforcement can track these predators are necessary. Smith is chair and Wasserman Schultz a member of the House Committee on the Judiciary.

As you read, consider the following questions:

1. According to the authors, what new challenge do parents face when social networking sites have replaced the play-ground?

2. What type of communication companies are already required to retain information to aid in the investigation of a crime, in the authors' opinion?

3. According to the viewpoint, what law enforcement leaders have testified that data retention is invaluable to investigating child pornography?

Just a few years ago, parents could rely on the four walls of their homes to keep their children safe. But in an age in which social networking sites have replaced the playground, parents face the new challenge of keeping their children safe from criminals who operate online.

While the Internet has proved to be of great value in many aspects of our lives, it has also become a vehicle for sex predators and pedophiles to distribute child pornography images and encourage others to engage in child pornography.

Child pornography may be the fastest-growing crime in America, increasing an average of 150 percent per year. The Justice Department estimates that there are now more than 1 million pornographic images of children on the Internet. The department also estimates that one-third of the world's pedophiles involved in organized child pornography rings live in the United States.

We must do more to keep our children safe from online sexual exploitation. That's why we have cosponsored H.R. 1981, the Protecting Children from Internet Pornographers Act. H.R. 1981 enables law enforcement officials to successfully locate and prosecute those who want to hurt our children.

Often, the only way to identify a pedophile who operates a website or exchanges child pornography images with other pedophiles is by an Internet protocol (IP) address. Law enforcement officials must obtain a subpoena and then request from the Internet service provider the name and address of the user of the IP address. Unfortunately, Internet service providers regularly purge these records, making it difficult, if not impossible, for investigators to apprehend child pornographers on the Internet.

H.R. 1981 directs Internet service providers to retain IP addresses longer in order to assist federal law enforcement officials with child pornography and other Internet investigations.

This narrow provision is specifically for the IP addresses the providers assign to their customers. It does not require the retention of any content, so the bill does not threaten any legitimate privacy interests of Internet users.

H.R. 1981 requires providers to retain these records for 12 months. This is less than an existing federal regulation that requires telephone companies to retain records for 18 months, including the name, address and telephone number of the caller, plus each phone number called and the date, time and length of the call.

If telephone companies are already required to retain certain information to aid in the investigation of a crime, why shouldn't Internet service providers be expected to do the same? In effect, this bill merely applies to the Internet what has applied to telephones for decades.

This is a commonsense bill that will make it possible for investigators to catch these criminals and at the same time, reduce child pornography on the Internet and spare thousands of children from being sexually exploited.

It is hard to believe that anyone would stand in the way of protecting our children from sexual predators. Yet there are

A Plea for Tools to Prosecute Online Child Pornographers

Online child exploitation presents challenges for both the Internet industry and law enforcement. However, . . . there is a way to balance the needs and priorities of both. Too many offenders have gone undetected by law enforcement and are willing to gamble that they can operate online anonymously. Federal, state, and local law enforcement have become more resourceful, but the lack of [Internet] connectivity retention [of data] presents a significant barrier to their investigations. Please help ensure that law enforcement has the tools they need to identify and prosecute those offenders who are misusing the Internet to victimize children. Too many child pornographers feel that they have found a sanctuary. Let's not prove them right.

Ernie Allen,
National Center for Missing & Exploited Children,
Testimony Before the US House of Representatives,
Committee on the Judiciary, Subcommittee on Crime,
Terrorism, and Homeland Security, "The Protecting
Children from Internet Pornographers Act," July 12, 2011.

some critics who contend that data retention is unnecessary because current law already requires Internet service providers to preserve records at the request of law enforcement agents for 90 days. But providers can only preserve the information they still have. By the time investigators discover the Internet child pornography and make the request under this provision, the provider has often already purged the IP address records.

Both Attorney General Eric Holder and FBI [Federal Bureau of Investigation] director Robert Mueller have testified that data retention is invaluable to investigating child pornography and other Internet-based crimes. And both Democratic and Republican administrations have called for data retention for a decade.

We will continue to work with stakeholders to make sure that the bill balances privacy concerns and the needs of Internet service providers. But we should all agree that more needs to be done to protect children from sexual predators.

Data retention is necessary to help track down and apprehend pedophiles who abuse children and destroy lives. Our children—the most innocent among us—deserve and need our help.

"While [the Protecting Children from Internet Pornographers Act of 2011] may have the best of intentions, its provisions are overzealous and would harm millions of Americans while doing little to stop child pornography."

Proposed Laws to Protect Children from Internet Pornographers Are Unconstitutional

Laura W. Murphy, Christopher Calabrese, and Jesselyn McCurdy

In the following viewpoint, Laura W. Murphy, Christopher Calabrese, and Jesselyn McCurdy assert that broad data retention laws that have little impact on child pornography are unconstitutional. Proposed data retention laws have no restrictions; thus law enforcement could use these records without probable cause, the authors claim. Moreover, Murphy and her colleagues argue, these laws create immunity from lawsuits that would compensate consumers for data breaches and privacy violations. In addition,

Laura W. Murphy, Christopher Calabrese, and Jesselyn McCurdy, "Letter from ACLU to Chairman Lamar Smith, U.S. House Judiciary Committee, RE: ACLU Urges Opposition to H.R. 1981 on Privacy and Internet Security," American Civil Liberties Union, July 20, 2011. Copyright © 2011 by the ACLU. All rights reserved. Reproduced by permission.

the authors maintain, proposed data retention laws allow for data requests without judicial scrutiny, thus trampling on American rights. Murphy is director and Calabrese and McCurdy are legislative counsel for the American Civil Liberties Union.

As you read, consider the following questions:

1. In the opinion of the authors, how did Maui police abuse IP address information?

2. Why do the authors claim it is important to note that the Electronic Communications Privacy Act was last updated in 1986?

3. In the authors' opinion, what could serve as a complete defense to any criminal or civil action brought against an Internet service provider?

On behalf of the American Civil Liberties Union (ACLU), a nonpartisan organization with more than a half million members, countless additional activists and supporters, and 53 affiliates nationwide dedicated to the principles of individual liberty and justice embodied in the U.S. Constitution, we are writing today to express our opposition to H.R. 1981, the "Protecting Children from Internet Pornographers Act of 2011" as modified by Chairman [Lamar] Smith's manager's amendment. We are specifically concerned with section 4 (retention of records), sections 5 and 6 (immunity provisions) and sections 7 and 11 (subpoenas authority). Collectively, these provisions invade the privacy of innocent individuals, create dangerous cybersecurity vulnerabilities and authorize overbroad information collection by law enforcement.

Sexual abuse of children is already a criminal act. All reasonable people agree that such abuse harms children to an almost unfathomable degree. Child pornography commercially exploits that harm. While H.R. 1981 may have the best of intentions, its provisions are overzealous and would harm millions of Americans while doing little to stop child pornography.

The Retention of Records

Section 4 of H.R. 1981 would impose sweeping requirements on Internet companies, forcing them to keep records on their customers for one full year—impacting hundreds of millions of Americans who have no connection whatsoever to the sexual exploitation of children. The legislation, as modified by the manager's amendment, would require that "a commercial provider of an electronic communication service shall retain for a period of at least one year a log of the temporarily assigned network addresses the provider assigns to a subscriber or customer of such service that enables the identification of the corresponding customer or subscriber information under subsection (c)(2) of this section." There is no limitation in the law requiring that these records be used in child exploitation cases. Instead, they would be available to law enforcement for any purpose.

Temporarily assigned network addresses, also known as IP [Internet protocol] addresses, can reveal very personal and private information. These addresses are the direct link between individuals and their online activity. In essence, an IP address is a proxy for an individual's name or other identifier online. Access to this link is the lynchpin in determining the sites users visit online—what their interests are, where they bank, what online accounts they have. While the use of such information has been limited to law enforcement by the amendment, the records still exist and can be illicitly accessed by hackers attempting to break into individual computers, or stalkers trying to find a particular person, or others with ill intent.

Access to records of IP addresses can reveal sensitive information. For example, police in Maui recently requested IP address information from a news website in order to identify a commenter in an article describing a particular case of police abuse. In other cases, law enforcement has sought the IP addresses of every visitor to a news site on a particular day.

Sweeping Effects on Privacy

Furthermore, many in law enforcement have argued that it is insufficient to retain information just from companies that assign IP addresses (such as Internet service providers). They argue that record retention should extend to others who provide e-mail and data storage services like Google, Facebook, and a wide swath of other Internet companies. Such a mandate would have even more sweeping effects on privacy.

Individual search results provide a good example of how detailed and invasive these types of records can be. For example, Google keeps temporarily assigned network addresses with each of its searches. If, as some have suggested, a record retention requirement is extended to service providers like Google, such searches would have to be kept for one year. Embarrassing searches on subjects like incontinence or depression, work-related searches for new clients, or inquiries about sensitive political or religious issues would all have to be retained.

Dated and Weak Laws

This proposal comes at a time when U.S. laws in the digital privacy area are woefully out of date. As the committee [the U.S. House Committee on the Judiciary] explored in multiple hearings last Congress, the Electronic Communications Privacy Act has not been substantially updated since 1986—before the creation of the World Wide Web. As the examples above demonstrate, the type and detail of records have increased dramatically since 1986. They have become much more revealing—describing reading habits, interests, personal relationships and a variety of other constitutionally protected interests—while rules for accessing and using these records have remained the same or, in the case of national security provisions, been weakened. The data retention mandate would exacerbate these problems, making records available and identifiable for even longer periods of time.

Perhaps worst of all, record-retention mandates do not address the main problems with investigating and prosecuting child pornography. In a recent report, the Government Accountability Office made clear that addressing the problem of child pornography is much more seriously hindered by:

- A lack of feedback to the National Center for Missing & Exploited Children (NCMEC) which results in incomplete or ineffective reports to law enforcement;

- The lack of a centralized "deconfliction" system that prevents multiple law enforcement entities from investigating the same crimes; and

- Backlogs in forensic analysis of digital evidence.

An increased record-retention mandate means adding even more records to a system that is already overburdened and ineffective.

The Immunity Provisions

Sections 5 and 6 are very expansive. While section 5 has been modified somewhat by the manager's amendment, we believe these provisions would still create immunity for companies that retain records pursuant to section 4 and exempt this collection from civil liability. As drafted, we believe these sections could overrule state data breach laws and data security protections as well as potentially immunize companies against tort and other claims.

The new section 2703(e) of title 18 would read:

No cause of action against a provider disclosing information under this chapter.—No cause of action shall lie in any court

An Invasive Proposal

Child pornography is certainly a substantial and difficult issue. But the data retention solution proposed in [the Protecting Children from Internet Pornographers Act of 2011] is overly expansive and invasive. This collection of user data will, in fact, create a new threat for millions of Internet users: the threat of dragnet law enforcement and data breaches. . . .

At a time of increasing security breaches and rising instances of identity theft, nothing could be worse than to unnecessarily collect vast amounts of information on Internet users without establishing appropriate and necessary safeguards for users.

Marc Rotenberg,
Testimony Before the House Committee on the Judiciary,
Subcommittee on Crime, Terrorism, and Homeland Security,
Hearing on H.R. 1981 the Protecting Children
from Internet Pornographers Act, July 12, 2011.

against any provider of wire or electronic communication service, its officers, employees, agents, or other specified persons *for retaining records*, providing information, facilities, or assistance in accordance with the terms of a court order, warrant, subpoena, statutory authorization, or certification under this chapter (new language in italics)

The breadth of this requirement is noteworthy. While under the new amendment language section 5 is now applicable only to IP address retention, such information is very sensitive and would still be harmful in the event of a data breach. Further, under the new section 6, a provider's good faith reliance on the need to retain records would serve as a complete defense to any criminal or civil action, whether brought under 18

USC 2707 (the civil liability provision of the Electronic Communications Privacy Act) or any other law. In practice, this means that any company that retains records pursuant to this section could argue that they are immune from any liability stemming from that retention. Even if poor data security practices lead to a data breach or mistakes lead to the loss of crucial data, the company would be immunized.

The sweeping nature of these immunity provisions would decrease corporate incentives to protect records and provide adequate data security. In a time when high-profile data breaches are daily news stories and identity theft is widespread, this provision seems ill-considered at best. Greater detail on this provision can be found in the July 12, 2011, testimony of Marc Rotenberg, director of the Electronic Privacy Information Center.

The Administrative Subpoena Grants Unchecked Authority

Sections 7 and 11 of H.R. 1981 create authority for the U.S. Marshals Service to issue administrative subpoenas "solely for the purpose of investigating 'unregistered' sex offenders." We oppose granting to the Marshals Service or any executive branch agency the power to issue subpoenas which would allow it to write its own search and disclosure orders with no judicial approval.

Under current law, the government can obtain documents or testimony through its normal criminal investigative powers, which include obtaining a criminal search warrant or grand jury subpoena. Criminal search warrants apply to all documents and require a judge or magistrate to find probable cause that the search will produce evidence of crime. Although grand jury subpoenas do not require probable cause, they do require a grand jury to find that the testimony or documents are relevant to an ongoing grand jury investigation of criminal activity and they can be challenged before a judge.

While administrative subpoenas are typically suited for regulatory investigations such as the administration of federal benefits programs, they have also been made available in certain criminal contexts where rigorous checks and balances provide protection against abuse. For decades, agencies such as the FBI [Federal Bureau of Investigation] have sought general administrative subpoena power and Congress has repeatedly been reluctant to grant it out of concern for the unchecked nature of such authority.

In addition, 18 U.S.C. 3486 currently grants the attorney general administrative subpoena authority in any investigation of a federal offense involving sexual exploitation or abuse of children. Since simple failure to maintain registry as a sex offender can be deemed such a federal offense, H.R. 1981 would in effect allow the Marshals Service to seize computer files of an unregistered sex offender without court approval even if he or she is not suspected of any new sex crime.

Americans still have a reasonable expectation that their federal government will not gather records about their day-to-day activities without probable cause of a crime and without a court order. We hope that Congress will protect the needs of law enforcement without sidestepping our Constitution's fundamental checks and balances. H.R. 1981 purports to restrain online child pornography, but in reality it fails to achieve that worthy objective while trampling the privacy rights of almost everyone who goes online. For these reasons, we oppose H.R. 1981 and urge the members of the committee to reject the bill or drastically reformulate sections 4, 5, 6, 7, and 11.

> *"The Stop Online Piracy Act ... would create new tools to target the worst-of-the-worst black markets."*

Brake the Internet Pirates: How to Slow Down Intellectual Property Theft in the Digital Era

Wall Street Journal

Online piracy of copyrighted and trademarked materials is a serious economic problem, claim the editors of the Wall Street Journal *in the following viewpoint. The Stop Online Piracy Act (SOPA) provides tools to specifically target online international pirates by allowing the US attorney general to sue foreign infringers, they maintain. Moreover, the editors assert, SOPA requires that website hosts take action against online pirates who use their sites. Some tech companies oppose SOPA, arguing that the law threatens Internet freedom, but creativity and innovation require protection to flourish, the editors reason. The* Wall Street Journal *is a widely read daily newspaper primarily covering financial and economic news and issues.*

As you read, consider the following questions:

1. According to the *Wall Street Journal* editors, why is it not surprising that President Barack Obama opposes SOPA?

2. How does SOPA version 3.0 address objections, in the authors' view?

3. What about the Internet do the authors believe makes it all the more important to police the abusers who hijack its architecture?

Wikipedia and many other websites are shutting down today to oppose a proposal in Congress on foreign Internet piracy, and the White House is seconding the protest. The covert lobbying war between Silicon Valley and most other companies in the business of intellectual property is now in the open, and this fight could define—or reinvent—copyright in the digital era.

Everyone agrees, or at least claims to agree, that the illegal sale of copyrighted and trademarked products has become a worldwide, multibillion-dollar industry and a legitimate and growing economic problem. This isn't college kids swapping MP3s, as in the 1990s. Rather, rogue websites set up shop overseas and sell U.S. consumers bootleg movies, TV shows, software, video games, books and music, as well as pharmaceuticals, cosmetics, fashion, jewelry and more.

Often consumers think they're buying copies or streams from legitimate retail enterprises, sometimes not. Either way, the technical term for this is theft.

The tech industry says it wants to stop such crimes, but it also calls any tangible effort to do so censorship that would "break the Internet." Wikipedia has never blacked itself out before on any other political issue, nor have websites like Mozilla or the social news aggregator Reddit. How's that for irony: Companies supposedly devoted to the free flow of in-

formation are gagging themselves, and the only practical effect will be to enable fraudsters. They've taken no comparable action against, say, Chinese repression.

Meanwhile, the White House let it be known over the weekend in a blog post—how fitting—that it won't support legislation that "reduces freedom of expression" or damages "the dynamic, innovative global Internet," as if this describes the reality of Internet theft. President Obama has finally found a regulation he doesn't like, which must mean that the campaign contributions of Google and the Stanford alumni club are paying dividends.

The House bill known as the Stop Online Piracy Act, or SOPA, and its Senate counterpart are far more modest than this cyber tantrum suggests. By our reading, they would create new tools to target the worst-of-the-worst black markets. The notion that a SOPA dragnet will catch a stray Facebook post or Twitter link is false.

Under the Digital Millennium Copyright Act of 1998, U.S. prosecutors and rights-holders can and do obtain warrants to shut down rogue websites and confiscate their domain names under asset-seizure laws. Such powers stop at the water's edge, however. SOPA is meant to target the international pirates that are currently beyond the reach of U.S. law.

The bill would allow the attorney general to sue infringers and requires the Justice Department to prove in court that a foreign site is dedicated to the wholesale violation of copyright under the same standards that apply to domestic sites. In rare circumstances, private plaintiffs can also sue for remedies, not for damages, and their legal tools are far more limited than the AG's.

If any such case succeeds after due process under federal civil procedure, SOPA requires third parties to make it harder to traffic in stolen online content. Search engines would be required to screen out links, just as they remove domestic piracy or child pornography sites from their indexes. Credit card and other online financial service companies couldn't complete transactions.

(Obligatory housekeeping: We at the *Journal* are in the intellectual property business, and our parent company, News Corp., supports the bills as do most other media content companies.)

Moreover, SOPA is already in its 3.0 version to address the major objections. Compromises have narrowed several vague and overly broad provisions. The bill's drafters also removed a feature requiring Internet service providers to filter the domain name system for thieves—which would have meant basically removing them from the Internet's phone book to deny consumer access. But the anti-SOPA activists don't care about these crucial details.

The e-vangelists seem to believe that anybody is entitled to access to any content at any time at no cost—open source. Their real ideological objection is to the concept of copyright itself, and they oppose any legal regime that values original creative work. The off-line analogue is Occupy Wall Street. [1]

Information and content may want to be free, or not, but that's for their owners to decide, not Movie2k.to or Library Pirate.me or MusicMP3.ru. The Founders recognized the economic benefits of intellectual property, which is why the Constitution tells Congress to "promote the Progress of Science and useful Arts by securing for limited Times to Authors and Inventors the exclusive Right to their respective Writings and Discoveries" (Article I, Section 8).

The Internet has been a tremendous engine for commercial and democratic exchange, but that makes it all the more important to police the abusers who hijack its architecture. SOPA merely adapts the current avenues of legal recourse for infringement and counterfeiting to new realities. Without rights that protect the creativity and innovation that bring fresh ideas and products to market, there will be far fewer ideas and products to steal.

---

1. Occupy Wall Street is a protest movement that began September 17, 2011, in New York City's Wall Street financial district. Protestors oppose social and economic inequality, high unemployment, greed, corruption, and the undue influence of corporations, particularly financial services, on government.

"*Sacrificing our ability to clearly send [the open Internet] message to the world, for the sake of making a purely symbolic gesture against piracy, would be a grotesque waste and a betrayal of our highest values.*"

The Stop Online Piracy Act Will Not Prevent Online Piracy

Julian Sanchez

The Stop Online Piracy Act (SOPA) would censor the Internet without stopping online pirates, argues Julian Sanchez in the following viewpoint. In fact, he claims, SOPA is simply another in a long line of ineffective efforts to stop online pirates. Unfortunately, Sanchez suggests, SOPA would block websites, discourage advertisers, and censor search engines based on administrative hearings without judicial review. Moreover, he maintains, vague, uncertain laws such as SOPA discourage investors and thus inhibit Internet markets, in turn slowing user safeguards. Sanchez, a research fellow at the CATO Institute, a libertarian think tank, was editor of the technology news site Ars Technica.

As you read, consider the following questions:

1. How will even the least technically sophisticated be able to bypass US-based blocking of pirate domains, according to Sanchez?

2. What will someone with an idea for the next YouTube have to explain to investors if laws such as SOPA are passed, in the author's opinion?

3. What do the government's own experts at the Sandia National Laboratories say about SOPA, in the author's view?

If the movie and music recording industries insist on adding to their already ample arsenal of weapons against online piracy, there are balanced proposals—like the OPEN Act[1] sponsored by Rep. Darrell Issa and Sen. Ron Wyden—worth considering. But creating a system of Internet censorship akin to China's "Great Internet Firewall"[2]—as contemplated by the Stop Online Piracy Act (SOPA) and its counterpart, PROTECT IP [Preventing Real Online Threats to Economic Creativity and Theft of Intellectual Property Act]—would do almost nothing to hamper true pirates, while threatening free speech, technological innovation, and global cybersecurity.

A Costly Speed Bump

The first thing to understand about SOPA is that it's just not going to work. Content industries have spent the past decade shutting down one pirate site or technology after another, and it's never been more than a speed bump for adaptive users.

1. The Online Protection and Enforcement of Digital Trade Act (OPEN Act) would stop transfers of money to foreign websites whose primary purpose is piracy or counterfeiting, whereas SOPA requires Internet providers and search engines to redirect users away from viewing the sites.
2. This is a nickname given to the Golden Shield Project, a censorship and surveillance project operated by the Ministry of Public Security (MPS) division of the government of the People's Republic of China.

Even the least technically sophisticated will be able to bypass U.S.-based blocking of supposed "pirate" domains by tweaking a simple browser setting, or installing a plug-in app [application], such as MAFIAAFire, with the click of a mouse. It is, as our own State Department says of Iran's "electronic curtain" around the Internet, a "very expensive endeavor" that is "bound to fail in today's increasingly interactive world." SOPA's virtual Maginot Line[3] will be burdensome to implement, but trivial to get around, making all the other harms it imposes a senseless waste—costs with no real compensating benefit.

Those costs, on the other hand, will be anything but trivial. More than a hundred eminent First Amendment scholars have condemned the silencing of legitimate, protected speech that SOPA will enable, as inevitable "collateral damage" of a measure as blunt and overbroad as the blocking of entire web domains. Our constitutional tradition clearly condemns the "prior restraint" of speech, even in the name of noble goals. In the context of obscenity law, our Supreme Court has held that "mere probable cause to believe a violation has transpired is not adequate to remove books or film from circulation . . . until the claimed justification for seizing such materials is properly established in an adversary proceeding."

A Threat to Free Speech

SOPA, however, would allow domains to be blocked, search engines to be censored, and advertisers forced to sever ties with sites—following a one-sided hearing subject to an even lower standard. Likely targets would include discussion forums where links to copyright infringing files might appear alongside protected First Amendment speech, as well as cyberlockers and other cloud storage services—popular among pi-

3. The Maginot Line was a line of fortifications that France constructed along its borders with Germany and Italy between 1930 and 1939. The fortification was strategically ineffective, as the Germans defeated the French army, completely sweeping by the line and conquering France in days. The name is used to recall a strategy or object that people hope will prove effective but instead fails miserably.

Who's Opposed to SOPA?

Much of the Internet industry and a large percentage of Internet users [are opposed to the Stop Online Piracy Act (SOPA)]. . . .

On November 15 [2011], Google, Facebook, Twitter, Zynga, eBay, Mozilla, Yahoo, AOL, and LinkedIn wrote a letter to key members of the U.S. Senate and House of Representatives, saying SOPA poses "a serious risk to our industry's continued track record of innovation and job creation, as well as to our nation's cybersecurity." . . .

A letter signed by Reps. Zoe Lofgren and Anna Eshoo, both California Democrats, and Rep. Ron Paul, the [2012] Republican presidential candidate from Texas, predicts that SOPA will invite "an explosion of innovation-killing lawsuits and litigation." Law professors have also raised concerns. And yes, there is a protest song.

Declan McCullagh,
"How SOPA Would Affect You: FAQ,"
CNET.com, January 18, 2012.

rates, but also wholly innocent users who would lose access to their legal files. Moreover, "anti-circumvention" language in the bill won't much worry foreign coders in league with pirates, but it could scare away programmers who build the vital anticensorship programs our own government has promoted as free speech tools for dissidents living under repressive governments.

Technology entrepreneurs are also opposed, because surveys suggest the massive uncertainty the law creates for overseas sites will be a powerful deterrent to the venture capitalists and angel investors that technology start-ups rely upon. Platforms for user-generated content like YouTube and Facebook have been key to the outpouring of creativity enabled by the Internet, though they also, inevitably, enable some copyright infringement as well. But someone with an idea for the next YouTube will have to explain to investors that the business risks being cut off from revenue and blocked for U.S. users if its American competitors are able to brand it as a "rogue" site. Bear in mind that the recording industry has already suggested it will go after "cloud storage" services, which allow users to access their own legally purchased and uploaded music from multiple devices, unless they're paid a cut.

Leaving Users Vulnerable

Equally disturbing, a who's-who of network engineers, including many of the creators of the modern Internet, have warned that tampering with the Domain Name System to enable blocking would upset the Internet's open architecture, and slow deployment of DNSSEC, a standard designed to safeguard network traffic against malicious hijacking by hackers. Former Department of Homeland Security assistant secretary Stewart Baker puts it bluntly: "SOPA will kill DNSSEC," leaving all Internet users more vulnerable. The government's own experts at the Sandia National Laboratories agree that SOPA is not only "unlikely to be effective," but will "negatively impact U.S. and global cybersecurity and Internet functionality."

The United States is not just the birthplace of the Internet: It has also long been one of the most vocal and consistent proponents of an open, unified global network, where no government firewall decides which sites citizens are allowed to see. Sacrificing our ability to clearly send that message to the world, for the sake of making a purely symbolic gesture against piracy, would be a grotesque waste and a betrayal of our highest values.

> "We should enable victims of cybercrime to sue the worst-of-the-worst hosting companies for the damage their crooked customers cause."

Internet Service Providers Should Be Held Liable for Cybercrime

Noah Shachtman

In the following viewpoint, Noah Shachtman argues that Internet service providers (ISPs) should be held liable for the crimes of the criminals that they host. Without the financial risk of liability, he asserts, ISPs have no incentive to stop doing business with paying criminal customers. If hosting criminals becomes costly, Shachtman claims, ISPs may be less willing to host them. Nevertheless, he reasons, liability should be limited to those known to regularly host criminals and only after these ISPs are given an opportunity to drop criminal customers. Shachtman, a contributing editor to the tech newsmagazine Wired *is a fellow at the Brookings Institution, a widely cited think tank.*

As you read, consider the following questions:

1. In Shachtman's view, which independent research group is a good source for a list of the worst hosting companies and networks?

2. To what types of hosting services will criminal customers turn to keep their content online no matter how many threats or complaints they receive, in the author's view?

3. In what way was the relationship between 18th- and 19th-century pirates and those states that sponsored them symbiotic, according to the author?

The best way to stop the tide of global cybercrime may be to sue the pants off of the hosting companies and Internet service providers [ISPs] online that are backing the crooks. . . . No one knows exactly how big the cybercrime underground is. But it is huge. According to the British government, online thieves, scammers, and industrial spies cost U.K. [United Kingdom] businesses an estimated $43.5 billion in the last year alone. Crooks for hire will infect a thousand computers for seven dollars—that's how simple it's become. 60,000 new malicious software variants are detected every day, thanks in part to a new breed of crimeware that makes stealing passwords about as hard as setting up a web page. Even the Pentagon's specialists are worried, noting in their new cybersecurity strategy that "the tools and techniques developed by cybercriminals are increasing in sophistication at an incredible rate."

Top U.S. officials keep bleating about a digital "Pearl Harbor." But if we're not careful, the Internet could be in danger of looking like the South Bronx, circa 1989—a place where crooks hold such sway that honest people find it hard to live or work there.

Targeting the Worst Hosting Companies

But there are ways to begin sidelining these crooks. First and foremost: Target the relatively small number of companies that support this massive criminal underground. There are more than 5,000 Internet service providers around the globe; according to the Organisation for Economic Co-operation and Development, half the world's spam traffic comes from just 50 ISPs. A recent study of mass e-mail campaigns showed that three payment companies processed 95 percent of the money those scams generated. When the Silicon Valley–based McColo hosting company was taken down, worldwide spam dropped 65 percent overnight.

These companies facilitate criminal enterprises, whether knowingly or not. And, unlike the criminals themselves—who hide behind disposable e-mail addresses and encrypted communications—it's no mystery who these firms are. The independent research group HostExploit, for example, pub-lishes a list of the worst-of-the-worst hosting companies and networks.

Yet Internet service providers and carrier networks that move data across the globe continue to do business with these crooked firms. There's no economic incentive to do otherwise. After all, the hosting company that caters to crooks also has legitimate customers, and both pay for Internet access.

Creating Incentives

So here's my idea for providing that incentive—turn the crimi-nal ecosystem on the scammers and thieves. We should enable victims of cybercrime to sue the worst-of-the-worst hosting companies for the damage their crooked customers cause. Here's how it might work:

- Take an independent list of bad hosts, like HostExploit's.

- Once the roster is published, a listed company would have some time (two weeks, say) to either drop their illicit customers—or explain why it doesn't belong in the rogues gallery.

- If the company complies (or explains itself sufficiently), then it is granted safe harbor from any lawsuit that might arise from the harm generated by the spammers, phishers [scammers who dupe e-mail users into revealing personal or confidential information], or botnet herders [individuals who breach the security of a collection of Internet-connected computers] it once helped.

- If the hosting company fails to comply, however, it becomes open to liability lawsuits. The company has already been warned that it's facilitating harmful activities and given a chance to correct its negligent behavior.

- If that same company ignores the warnings and appears on the worst-of-the-worst list again, the firm's ISP should also be liable. (Of course, the provider should be given at least as much time and opportunity to address the problem.)

For the plan to make any kind of sense, the publisher of the rogues gallery would have to be crystal clear about how it reached its conclusions—and what a company could do to get itself off. The list could only cover a few universally recognized crimes, like theft, fraud, and criminal trespass. In other words: This wouldn't work for politically inflammatory speech or copyright infringement; they're too open to abuse and overly broad interpretation. And because the legal precedents are so confusing, it'll probably take an act of Congress to put it all in place (a tall order, considering those jokers can't even figure out a way to pay our debts).

Even if that happens, this plan won't help in all cases. Crooks will still be able to turn to so-called "bulletproof hosting" services, which promise to keep customers' content online no matter how many threats or complaints are received. Or they can relocate to hosting companies in places like China and Russia. Still, the United States isn't such a bad place to start. 20 of HostExploit's 50 worst are American.

Such a system gives ISPs enormous incentives to disconnect criminally connected hosts, even if it means a temporary dip in revenue. Unlike a lot of the plans making their way through Congress (or already on the books), this one provides a clear standard for bad behavior and a clear path for leaving the rogues gallery. It applies pressure on the broader ISP community to weed out the worst of the worst—without heavy-handed government intervention.

Finding Historical Parallels

In my year of research for this [viewpoint], I kept finding parallels between modern cybercrime and piracy of the 18th and 19th centuries. Both were pervasive. Both were seemingly beyond the reach of the law. Both were employed by individual crooks as well as big state militaries. Both relied on their economic support systems.

"In all of the notable eras of piracy," University of South Carolina historian Donald Puchala writes, "relationships between pirates and those who abetted their projects amounted in effect to conspiracies of greed. The relationships were symbiotic: Pirates could neither accomplish their ends nor convert their booty into profits without the aid of their protectors; for their part, the protectors could not so readily and splendidly enrich themselves without the booty brought in by the pirates."

One of the turning points in global attitudes toward piracy occurred when pirates began to threaten the economic interests of the states that previously sponsored them. The pirates picked fights with allies, hijacked friendly ships, and, as a result, made new enemies in cities like London and Paris. And when the governments decided to definitively retaliate, one of the first steps they took was to shut down the markets for pirate booty. The most effective way to target the hijackers was through their economic support system.

Maybe there's a chance of seeing a similar shift online. If ISPs start seeing rogue hosting companies as financial time bombs instead of as paying customers, it would represent a huge step forward in marginalizing cybercriminals globally. For that to happen, some hosts may have to go to court.

"[Allowing cybercrime victims to sue Internet service providers] wouldn't solve the problem it seeks to deal with . . . and (even worse) it would open up all sorts of collateral damage or unintended consequences."

Making Internet Service Providers Liable Will Not Reduce Cybercrime

Mike Masnick

Making Internet service providers (ISPs) liable for crimes committed by their customers would not stop online crime, claims Mike Masnick in the following viewpoint. Internet criminals would simply find hosts elsewhere, he asserts. Moreover, Masnick maintains, expanding third-party liability policies to ISPs might encourage policy makers to extend liability for less serious crimes such as copyright infringement. He reasons that the best way to discourage crime is to target those responsible—the criminals themselves—and use shaming techniques to put criminal websites out of business. Masnick, founder and chief executive officer of Floor64, an Internet platform innovation company, is editor of the Techdirt *blog.*

As you read, consider the following questions:

1. What does Masnick acknowledge about Noah Shachtman's paper recommending third-party liability as a tool to fight cybercrime?

2. What has the entertainment industry been dreaming about for over a decade, in the author's opinion?

3. In the author's view, how should public pressure be applied to ISPs?

L et me start off this post by noting that, while I don't know Noah Shachtman personally (other than a few e-mails back and forth many years ago), I've always liked his work writing for *Wired* and other publications. However, I'm surprised to see him advocating the strong use of third-party liability as a tool to deal with cybercrime, as a part of a paper for the Brookings Institution. The idea is that, when talking about spammers & scammers online, there are, perhaps, a small number of ISPs [Internet service providers] who tend to do business with these guys, and Shachtman believes that by making those ISPs liable, it would pressure them into cutting off the bad clients.

Shachtman has numerous caveats and is pretty specific in his plan that it only apply to a specific list put out by a trusted independent third party, that the methodology for being on the list is clear and that an appeals process also be explicit. On top of that, he says that it should be limited to "universally recognized crimes, like theft, fraud, and criminal trespass" and is clear in saying that it "wouldn't work for politically inflammatory speech or copyright infringement; they're too open to abuse and overly broad interpretation."

A Bad Idea

Also, in reading the report, it's clear that this isn't just something he came up with overnight, or some random blogger or reporter dashing off a column on some fragment of a thought

Responsibility Must Lie at the Internet's Edges

The Internet is dumb. It only does one thing: route packets of information wherever they say they should go. This dumb, ingenious network allows far cheaper, faster transmission of text, images, data, sound, video, and two-way voice. What makes the network ingenious is that all the smarts and power lie at the edges.

Internet policy must follow the design of the Internet itself. Just as the computing power lies at the edges of the Internet, so too must the responsibility. To the maximum extent possible, responsibility for wrongdoing must stay with wrongdoers. Responsibility for protection must stay at the edges with users.

Jim Harper, "Against ISP Liability,"
Regulation, *Spring 2005.*

they had an hour before deadline. He's put a lot of thought and research into this. But I still think the idea is dreadful and shortsighted. It wouldn't solve the problem it seeks to deal with, at all, and (even worse) it would open up all sorts of collateral damage or unintended consequences.

First off, it wouldn't solve the problem it's trying to solve. We've seen this time and time again with attempts to shut down any kind of "rogue" behavior online by going after intermediaries. The bad players just figure out some other place to go, and they often go further underground in ways that makes it tougher to find or track them and their activities. Even Shachtman admits that many would likely jump to ISPs elsewhere. So, if it's not actually stopping the behavior, then what's the value?

Second, while Shachtman is clear that this shouldn't be used for those other things, chipping away at third-party liability protections in any arena is quite dangerous, because it's not hard to see lobbyists using that to push for such rules to be expanded to cover *their* pet area. Anyone who thinks that the RIAA [Recording Industry Association of America] and MPAA [Motion Picture Association of America] wouldn't pounce on this and work hard to add copyright infringement to the list simply hasn't been paying attention. What Shachtman describes in terms of the ability to sue an ISP for third-party actions has been the legacy entertainment industry's . . . dream for over a decade. Anyone who thinks that politicians would distinguish the types of crimes that Shachtman focuses on from garden variety claims of copyright infringement is living in a dream world.

More Effective Solutions

And, honestly, I'm still at a loss as to why this is actually needed. It seems like there remain much more effective ways to deal with issues like this that don't involve giving up basic concepts of properly applying liability to the actual party responsible. The first is actually targeting *those responsible* for the crimes. If they're using known ISPs, then it seems like there is a record trail that can be traced back to go after those actually breaking the law to try to put them out of business. Second, if the concern (as it appears) is that some US ISPs are doing this, and that's a shame, then deal with that publicly, by more publicly shaming ISPs who are popular among criminals. Use public pressure to get them to (a) either help law enforcement or (b) to enforce reasonable terms of service. Trying to make them liable as a third party will make life difficult for them, but not the actual scammers.

Periodical and Internet Sources Bibliography

The following articles have been selected to supplement the diverse views presented in this chapter.

Sandra Aistars	"OPEN Act Falls Short for Artists and Creators," *Huffington Post*, December 15, 2011. www.huffingtonpost.com.
Chloe Albanesius	"Will Online Piracy Bill Combat 'Rogue' Web Sites or Cripple the Internet?," *PC Magazine*, November 1, 2011.
Al Franken	"The Most Important Free Speech Issue of Our Time," *Huffington Post*, December 20, 2010. www.huffingtonpost.com.
Andrew Keen	"The Death of the Internet Has Been Greatly Exaggerated," TechCrunch, November 14, 2011. http://techcrunch.com.
Stephen J. Lukasik	"Protecting Users of the Cyber Commons," *Communications of the ACM*, September 2011.
Rebecca MacKinnon	"Let's Take Back the Internet!," *Huffington Post*, December 7, 2011. www.huffingtonpost.com.
Wayne Rash	"House SOPA Hearings Reveal Anti-Internet Bias on Committee, Witness List," eWeek.com, November 16, 2011.
Fahmida Y. Rashid	"Google, Tech Giants, Free Speech Advocates Oppose House Online Piracy Bill," eWeek.com, November 16, 2011.
Aliya Sternstein	"Apparent Wave of Cyber Breaches Is an Illusion," NextGov.com, July 1, 2011.
Matt Welch	"Washington Attempts to Make Us All Culpable for Online Child Pornography," *Reason*, July 12, 2011.

For Further Discussion

Chapter 1

1. Sid Kirchheimer claims that identity theft is a serious problem for American consumers. Lynn Langton and Michael Planty argue, on the other hand, that for most victims, the impact of identity theft is small. What types of evidence do the authors use to support their claims? Which do you find more convincing? Explain.

2. According to John R. Rossi, cyberterrorism is a serious problem that poses a threat to America's infrastructure systems. Maura Conway counters that the probability of a serious cyberterrorist threat is small. The authors have different views on the skill level, goals, and motives of terrorists. How do these differing views influence the authors' arguments? Which do you believe is more persuasive? Explain.

3. Stephen E. Siwek claims that music piracy poses a serious threat to the music and its interdependent industries. Eric Bangeman disagrees, arguing that an accurate economic analysis of music piracy must take into account the realities of the digital marketplace. Which viewpoint do you find more persuasive? Explain.

4. What commonalities can you find in the rhetoric used by the authors on both sides of the debates in this chapter? Explain, citing examples from the texts.

Chapter 2

1. Kim Hone-McMahan maintains that predators use online social media to exploit young, vulnerable users. Steve Rendall, however, claims that the media hype about online predators is largely inaccurate and exploits fear for profit.

How do the rhetorical strategies of each author differ? Which strategy do you find more persuasive? Explain.

2. According to the authors of the viewpoints in this chapter, cybercriminals use different online media in different ways. What are some of the characteristics of these media that make particular types of cybercrime possible? Which media do you think make people most vulnerable? Explain, providing illustrative examples.

3. The authors in this chapter have different ideas about the function and purpose of social media. How are these differences reflected in their views on how cybercriminals use online media to commit crime? Explain, citing examples from the texts.

Chapter 3

1. John Feffer argues that diplomacy requires some secrecy; thus transparency activist organizations such as WikiLeaks that expose comments made by participants threaten diplomatic negotiations that impact American security. David Carr agrees that governments need to keep some secrets; however, he believes that transparency activists such as WikiLeaks serve a legitimate journalistic function. How do the authors' affiliations influence their arguments? Does this affect whether one viewpoint is more persuasive? Explain.

2. Peter Ludlow claims that Internet hacktivists use their hacking skills as a way to express their political views. Charles Arthur asserts that hacktivists behave more like a mob of protesters. Ludlow believes the size and anonymity of these networks make them effective because they are difficult to oppose or expose. Arthur believes that these same characteristics are a disadvantage, as hacktivist networks lack organization or rules of political engagement.

Which view of hacktivist organizations do you believe is more accurate? Explain, citing evidence from the viewpoints.

3. Tim Hwang maintains that Internet activism reflects a long war over who should control the Internet. Some hackers claim that the Internet should be completely open and transparent, and that they should use their hacking skills to oppose those who believe that the Internet should be subject to regulation and control by governments. Hwang concludes that because people with a strong interest in freedom developed the Internet and those who favor openness are growing in number, they are perhaps undefeatable. Do you agree, or are corporate, government, and public interests too strong? Explain.

4. How do the affiliations of the authors in this chapter influence their rhetoric? What type of rhetoric do you find most persuasive? Explain, citing examples from the viewpoints.

Chapter 4

1. What commonalities can you find in the rhetoric used by the authors in both sides of the debate over what laws will prevent cybercrime? Which strategies do you think are most persuasive? Explain, citing examples from the texts.

2. Andrew Crocker claims that since companies remain reluctant to disclose data breaches to consumers, a national disclosure standard is necessary. William H. Saito claims that regulation stifles innovation and limits consumer choice and should thus be avoided. He suggests that companies better inform consumers of the vulnerabilities inherent in modern technologies and take strong steps to protect data. What evidence does each author provide to support his claim? Which do you find more persuasive? Explain.

3. Lamar Smith and Debbie Wasserman Schultz believe predators who exploit children online are a serious problem that requires legislation to make it easier to track and apprehend child pornographers. Laura W. Murphy, Christopher Calabrese, and Jesselyn McCurdy argue that these laws are too broad and will lead to unconstitutional violations of civil liberties. How do the affiliations, the rhetorical strategies, and the evidence offered by the authors differ? Which view do you find more persuasive? Explain.

4. *Wall Street Journal* editors claim that the Stop Online Piracy Act (SOPA) is necessary to address the problem of online piracy. Julian Sanchez claims that not only will the act not stop online piracy, but SOPA will also lead to censorship. The *Wall Street Journal* sees the law as a way to protect creativity, while Sanchez believes the law stifles creativity. Does any argument or evidence in either viewpoint effectively address the competing view of creativity in the opposing view? Explain.

5. Noah Shachtman maintains that holding Internet service providers (ISPs) liable for their crimes will motivate ISPs not to host cybercriminals. Mike Masnick disputes this claim, arguing that Internet criminals will just go elsewhere and that laws should target criminals, not ISPs. How does the rhetoric of the two authors differ? Which strategy do you find more persuasive? Explain.

Organizations to Contact

The editors have compiled the following list of organizations concerned with the issues debated in this book. The descriptions are derived from materials provided by the organizations. All have publications or information available for interested readers. The list was compiled on the date of publication of the present volume; the information provided here may change. Be aware that many organizations take several weeks or longer to respond to inquiries, so allow as much time as possible.

American Civil Liberties Union (ACLU)
125 Broad Street, 18th Floor, New York, NY   10004
(212) 549-2500
website: www.aclu.org

The American Civil Liberties Union (ACLU) works to uphold civil rights and liberties, focusing specifically on rights such as free speech, equal protection, due process, and privacy. The ACLU takes on court cases that address and whose rulings define these civil rights and liberties; in recent years, many ACLU court cases have addressed issues such as Internet censorship and privacy. Backgrounders such as "2011 Cybersecurity Legislative Proposals," reports such as "Nationwide Cell Phone Tracking Public Records Request: Findings and Analysis," and links to ACLU op-eds such as "The Patriot Act Was Just the Start: 10 Years of Unrestrained Surveillance" are available on the website.

Berkman Center for Internet & Society
23 Everett Street, 2nd Floor, Cambridge, MA   02138
(617) 495-7547 • fax: (617) 495-7641
e-mail: cyber@law.harvard.edu
website: http://cyber.law.harvard.edu

The Berkman Center for Internet & Society conducts research on legal, technical, and social developments in cyberspace and assesses the need for laws and sanctions. The center publishes a monthly newsletter, blog posts, and articles based on its research efforts, many of which are available on its website, including "2010 Report on Distributed Denial of Service (DDoS) Attacks, Enhancing Child Safety and Online Technologies" and "Youth, Creativity, and Copyright in the Digital Age."

Cato Institute

1000 Massachusetts Avenue NW
Washington, DC   20001-5403
(202) 842-0200 • fax: (202) 842-3490
e-mail: cato@cato.org
website: www.cato.org

The Cato Institute is a libertarian public policy research foundation that aims to limit the role of government and protect civil liberties. The institute publishes the quarterlies *CATO Journal* and *Regulation* and the bimonthly *Cato Policy Report*. Its website publishes selections from these and other publications, including "The Durable Internet: Preserving Network Neutrality Without Regulation," "SOPA, Internet Regulation and the Economics of Piracy," "Consumer Online Privacy," and "Everybody Wants to Rule the Web."

Center for Democracy & Technology (CDT)

1634 I Street NW, #1100, Washington, DC   20006
(202) 637-9800 • fax: 202-637-0968
website: www.cdt.org

The Center for Democracy & Technology (CDT) works to ensure that regulations concerning all current and emerging forms of technology are in accordance with democratic values, especially free expression and privacy. The center works to promote its ideals through research and education, as well as through grassroots movements. On its website, CDT publishes articles, papers, reports, and testimony, including "PIPA/SOPA and the Online Tsunami: A First Draft of the Future," "Alternate Ways to Fight Internet Piracy," and "Can the Internet Remain Open for Everyone?"

Computer Crime and Intellectual Property Section (CCIPS)
US Department of Justice, 950 Pennsylvania Avenue NW
Washington, DC   20530-0001
(202) 514-2000
e-mail: AskDOJ@usdoj.gov
website: http://www.justice.gov/criminal/cybercrime/

The Computer Crime and Intellectual Property Section (CCIPS) of the US Department of Justice is responsible for implementing national strategies to combat computer and intellectual property crimes worldwide. CCIPS works with other government agencies, the private sector, academic institutions, and foreign counterparts. CCIPS attorneys run complex investigations, resolve unique legal and investigative issues raised by emerging computer and telecommunications technologies, and litigate cases. In addition, CCIPS trains law enforcement personnel, comments on and proposes legislation, and initiates and participates in international efforts to combat computer and intellectual property crime. Publications, primarily designed for those prosecuting crimes, include manuals for prosecuting cybercrimes and forensic methodology. On its website are reports on recent efforts to protect intellectual property, such as "IP Enforcement Coordinator's 2010 Annual Report."

Electronic Frontier Foundation (EFF)
454 Shotwell Street, San Francisco, CA   94110-1914
(415) 436-9333 • fax: (415) 436-9993
e-mail: info@eff.org
website: www.eff.org

The Electronic Frontier Foundation (EFF) is an organization that aims to promote a better understanding of telecommunications issues. It fosters awareness of civil liberties issues arising from advancements in computer-based communications media and supports litigation to preserve, protect, and extend First Amendment rights in computing and telecommunications technologies. EFF's publications include the quarterly newsletter *Networks & Policy*, the biweekly electronic newsletter *EFFector Online*, and white papers and articles, including "Unintended Consequences: Twelve Years Under the DMCA," "Hollywood's New War on Software Freedom and Internet Innovation," "Human Rights and Technology Sales: How Corporations Can Avoid Assisting Repressive Regimes," and "Hacktivists in the Frontline Battle for the Internet."

Embracing Digital Youth

474 W. Twenty-Ninth Avenue, Eugene, OR   97405
(541) 556-1145
e-mail: info@embracingdigitalyouth.org
website: www.embracingdigitalyouth.org

Embracing Digital Youth, formerly the Center for Safe and Responsible Internet Use, is dedicated to educating parents, educators, and policy makers about the most effective methods of encouraging safe and responsible Internet use by children and teens. The group emphasizes the importance of equipping youth with the knowledge and personal strength to make good decisions that will keep them out of potentially harmful situations when using the Internet. Copies of articles, issue briefs, and reports are available on its website, including "Cyberbullying, Sexting & Predators, Oh My!," "Addressing Youth Risk in the Digital Age in a Positive and Restorative Manner," "A Web 2.0 Approach to Internet Safety: Prevention and Intervention," and "Social Networking Technologies: Here to Stay and It's Really Okay."

Federal Bureau of Investigation (FBI)

935 Pennsylvania Avenue NW, Washington, DC   20535-0001
(202) 324-3000
website: www.fbi.gov/about-us/investigate/cyber/cyber

The Federal Bureau of Investigation (FBI) is the nation's law enforcement agency. One of its areas of investigation is cybercrime. The FBI's Cyber Crime website link includes analysis of its priorities, explanations of the latest cyber threats and scams, recent cases and prosecutions, and strategies to help citizens protect themselves and report incidents. The Cyber Crime website administers a number of programs related to cybersecurity and offers cybersecurity resources for businesses and individuals.

Federal Trade Commission
Consumer Response Center, 600 Pennsylvania Avenue NW
Washington, DC   20580
(202) 326-2222
website: www.ftc.gov/bcp/edu/microsites/idtheft/

The Federal Trade Commission's identify theft website is a resource for consumers, businesses, and law enforcement to learn about the crime of identity theft. On the website, consumers can learn how to avoid identity theft and what to do if their identity is stolen, businesses can learn how to prevent problems and help their customers deal with identity theft, and law enforcement can find resources to help victims of identity theft. Publications on the website's Consumer Publications link include the articles "Talking About Identify Theft: A How-to-Guide," "What's Behind Ads for a New Credit Identity?," and "How Not to Get Hooked by a Phishing Scam." The website Reference Desk provides links to laws, reports, and testimony on identity theft issues.

Free Software Foundation (FSF)
51 Franklin Street, Fifth Floor, Boston, MA   02110-1301
(617) 542-5942
website: www.fsf.org

The Free Software Foundation (FSF), founded by hacker Richard Stallman, advocates the development and use of free software with open-source code. The foundation believes dominance of company-owned, proprietary software such as Microsoft Windows threaten individual liberties. FSF asserts that software should not be controlled by proprietary software companies or governments that might seek to restrict and monitor others. Instead, the foundation claims that people should have control over the technology they use in their homes, schools, and businesses, where computers work for our individual and communal benefit. FSF sponsors the GNU Project, an ongoing effort to provide a complete operating system licensed as free software. A description of GNU is available on its website. Also on its website, FSF maintains a library of articles covering free software philosophy.

Pew Internet & American Life Project
1615 L Street NW, Suite 700, Washington, DC   20036
(202) 419-4500 • fax: (202) 419-4505
e-mail: info@pewinternet.org
website: www.pewinternet.org

The Pew Internet & American Life Project is an initiative of the Pew Research Center. The project explores the impact of the Internet on children, families, communities, the workplace, schools, health care, and civic/political life. Pew Internet provides data and analysis on Internet usage and its effects on American society. On its website, the project provides access to articles and reports, including "Parting with Privacy with a Quick Click," "Reputation and Social Media, State of Music Online: Ten Years After Napster," and "Privacy Management on Social Media Sites."

Recording Industry Association of America (RIAA)
1025 F Street NW, 10th Floor, Washington, DC   20004
(202) 775-0101
website: www.riaa.com

The Recording Industry Association of America (RIAA) is a trade group that represents the US recording industry. Its mission is to foster a business and legal climate that supports and promotes its members' creative and financial vitality. RIAA works to protect intellectual property rights worldwide and the First Amendment rights of artists. It conducts consumer, industry, and technical research, as well as monitors and reviews state and federal laws, regulations, and policies. In addition to a list of legal online music downloading services, its website explains the nature and scope of online and street piracy and publishes downloadable leaflets such as "Music and the Internet" for parents and students.

WiredSafety

96 Linwood Plaza, #417, Ft. Lee, NJ   07024-3701
(201) 463-8663
e-mail: askparry@wiredsafety.org
website: www.wiredsafety.org

Operating online since 1995, WiredSafety is an Internet patrol organization that not only monitors the web for safety violations but also provides education on all aspects of Internet safety. Volunteers worldwide offer their time and are the driving force of the organization. The WiredSafety website provides information categorized by online concern and by technology type and is specialized for parents, educators, law enforcement, and youth. Links to issue- and age-specific projects such as Teenangels and StopCyberbullying are also available on the website.

Bibliography of Books

Susan W. Brenner   *Cybercrime: Criminal Threats from Cyberspace.* Westport, CT: Praeger, 2010.

Jeffrey Carr   *Inside Cyber Warfare.* Sebastopol, CA: O'Reilly, 2012.

Julia Davidson and Petter Gottschalk, eds.   *Internet Child Abuse: Current Research and Policy.* New York: Routledge, 2011.

Johan Eriksson and Giampiero Giacomello, eds.   *International Relations and Security in the Digital Age.* New York: Routledge, 2007.

Charles Fairchild   *Pop Idols and Pirates: Mechanisms of Consumption and the Global Circulation of Popular Music.* Burlington, VT: Ashgate, 2008.

Jack Goldsmith and Tim Wu   *Who Controls the Internet?: Illusions of a Borderless World.* New York: Oxford University Press, 2008.

Emmanuel Goldstein   *The Best of 2600: A Hacker Odyssey.* Indianapolis, IN: Wiley, 2008.

Seymour E. Goodman and Herbert S. Lin, eds.   *Toward a Safer and More Secure Cyberspace.* Washington, DC: National Academies Press, 2007.

Joseph Harrison   *Identity Theft.* Baltimore, MD: Waywiser Press, 2008.

K. Jaishankar, ed. *Cyber Criminology: Exploring Internet Crimes and Criminal Behavior.* Boca Raton, FL: CRC Press, 2011.

Andrew Keen *The Cult of the Amateur: How Today's Internet Is Killing Our Culture.* New York: Doubleday, 2007.

Joseph M. Kizza and Florence M. Kizza *Securing the Information Infrastructure.* Hershey, PA: Cybertech, 2008.

Sharon Kleinman, ed. *Displacing Place: Mobile Communication in the Twenty-First Century.* New York: Peter Lang, 2007.

Robin M. Kowalski, Susan P. Limber, and Patricia W. Agatston *Cyber Bullying: Bullying in the Digital Age.* Malden, MA: Blackwell, 2008.

Greg Lastowka *Virtual Justice: The New Laws of Online Worlds.* New Haven, CT: Yale University Press, 2010.

Steven Levy *Hackers: Heroes of the Computer Revolution.* Sebastopol, CA: O'Reilly, 2010.

Martin C. Libicki *Conquest in Cyberspace: National Security and Information Warfare.* New York: Cambridge University Press, 2007.

Martin C. Libicki *Cyberdeterrence and Cyberwar.* Santa Monica, CA: RAND, 2009.

Joseph Menn — *Fatal System Error: The Hunt for the New Crime Lords Who Are Bringing Down the Internet.* New York: Public Affairs, 2010.

William A. Owens, Kenneth W. Dam, and Herbert S. Lin, eds. — *Technology, Policy, Law, and Ethics Regarding U.S. Acquisition and Use of Cyberattack Capabilities.* Washington, DC: National Academies Press, 2009.

T.F. Peterson — *Nightwork: A History of Hacks and Pranks at MIT.* Cambridge, MA: MIT Press, 2011.

Kevin Poulsen — *Kingpin: How One Hacker Took Over the Billion-Dollar Cybercrime Underground.* New York: Crown, 2011.

Johann Rost and Robert L. Glass — *The Dark Side of Software Engineering: Evil on Computing Projects.* Hoboken, NJ: Wiley, 2011.

Julian Sher — *Caught in the Web: Inside the Police Hunt to Rescue Children from Online Predators.* New York: Carroll & Graf, 2007.

Daniel J. Solove — *The Future of Reputation: Gossip, Rumor, and Privacy on the Internet.* New Haven, CT: Yale University Press, 2007.

David S. Wall — *Cybercrime: The Transformation of Crime in the Information Age.* Malden, MA: Polity Press, 2007.

Nancy E. Willard   *Cyberbullying and Cyberthreats:*
Responding to the Challenge of Online
Social Aggression, Threats, and
Distress. Champaign, IL: Research
Press, 2007.

Index

A

Academic computer and information security, 168

ACS:Law (website), 137

Activism. *See* Hacktivism; Protests

Advertising
Facebook, 87, 89, 91
Stop Online Piracy Act effects, 193, 195
vending machines, 172

Afghanistan Conflict (2001-), WikiLeaks coverage, 110, 116–117, 124–125

Airline terrorism, 52–53

al Qaeda, 45

Allen, Ernie, 178

Amazon.com, 119

American Civil Liberties Union (ACLU), 181

Amnesty International, 128

Anonymity
anonymous speech, protections, 72
Chinese Internet user programs and projects, 148–149
as counter to terrorist ideology, 47, 53
false online identities, 98, 101, 102, 134
hacktivist values and violations, 130, 132
nature of hacking, 14

Anonymous (hacker group), 18, 136
Church of Scientology activism, 122, 126–127, 136
corruption and criticisms, 130, 132–134, 136–139
credit card sites attacks, 136–137, 142
hacktivism actions denied, 131–132
Iran election activism, 127
member demographics, 133, 138
San Francisco Bay Area Rapid Transit activism, 18–19, 132–133

Anti-virus programs, 89, 135, 167

Arab Spring protests, 2011, 127, 136

Arquilla, John, 158

Arrests
bloggers, China, 148
extortion, 78
flash mob crime, 96, 97
fraud, 16, 27
hacktivists, 125, 133, 134, 142
online predators, 78
scam victims, 27–28, 29

Arthur, Charles, 130–139

Assange, Julian
imprisonment and insurance, 120, 124–125
as one of many hacktivists, 123–124, 129, 141–142, 144
philosophy, 118, 119, 128, 144
WikiLeaks leadership, 117, 118, 120, 123–125

Assumed identity
deceased persons, 25
hacktivist leaders, 134

N